DUNGEON BUILDER

DUNGEON PLANNER WITH 50 PREMADE DUNGEON MAPS FOR TABLETOP ROLEPLAYING GAMES.

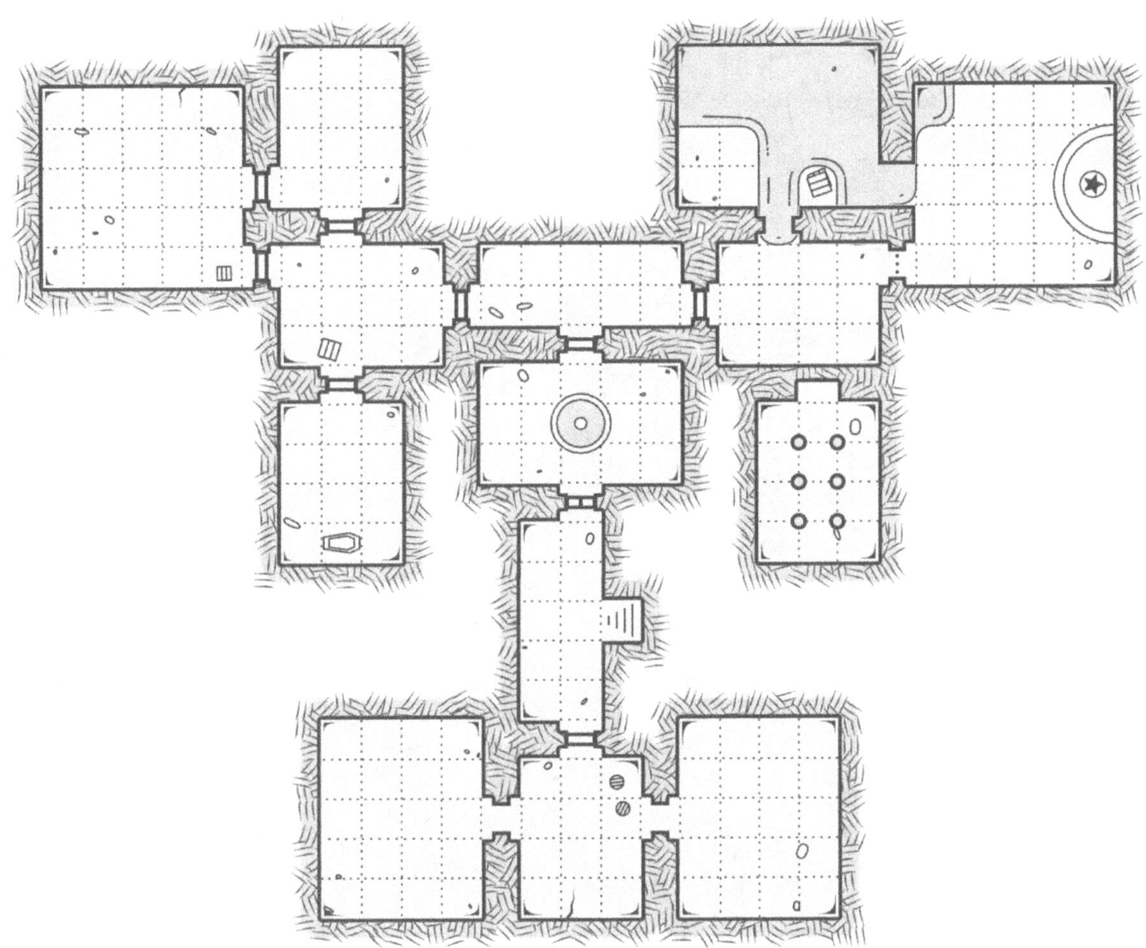

VOLUME 1

All dungeons made by watawatabou dungeon generator.

Please consider supporting his work at patreon.com/watawatabou/

Forsaken Labyrinth of Spirits

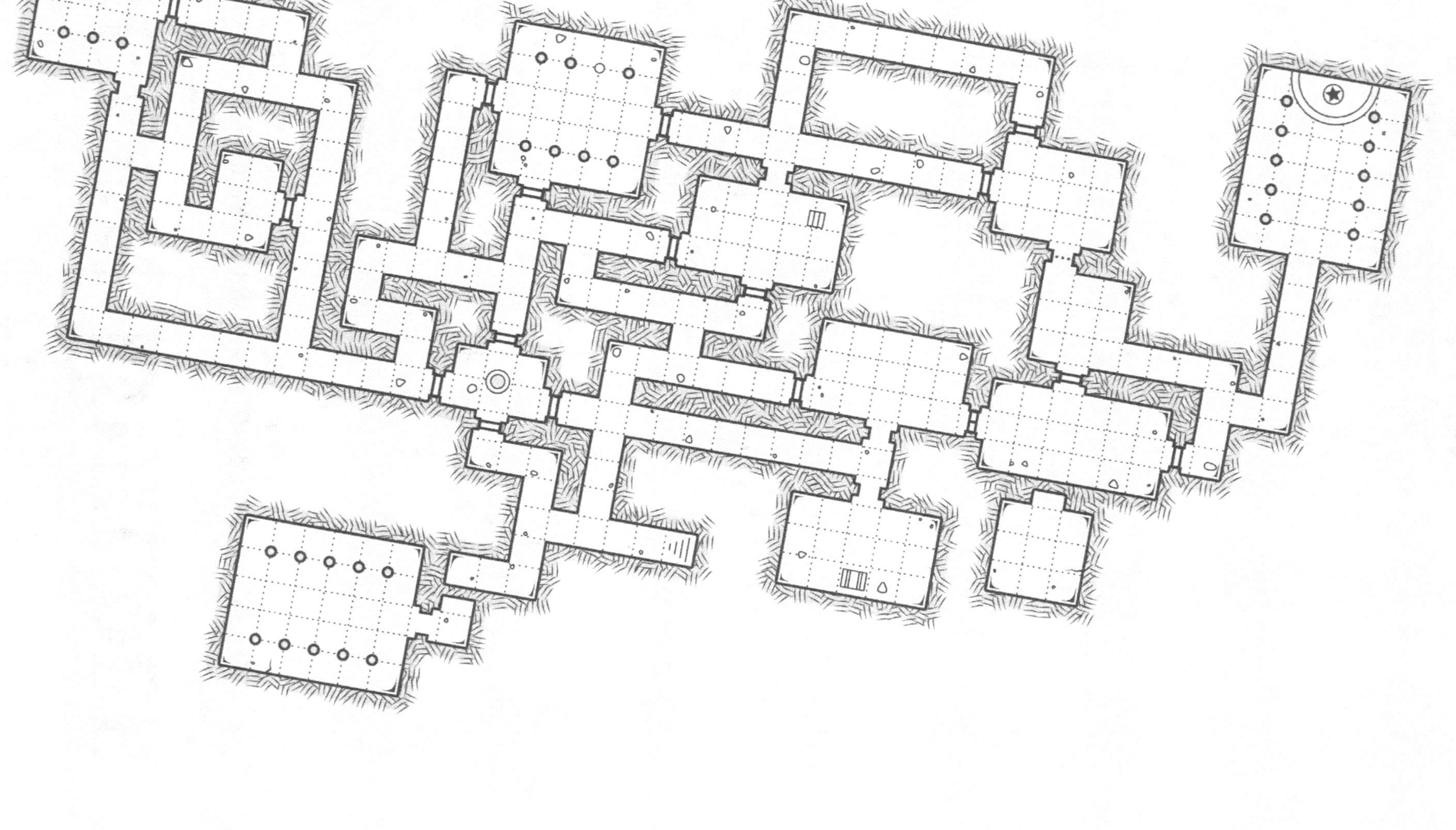

The labyrinth is situated deep in the jungle, far from civilization. Recently a band of goblins rediscovered it.

Location: Faction:

Illumination: Temperature:

Architecture:

Plot Hook:

History:

Inhabitants:

Points of Interest:

Stronghold of Rage Lily

After being destroyed by a great earthquake decades ago the stronghold remained uninhabited. Currently it is badly infested by sparrows.

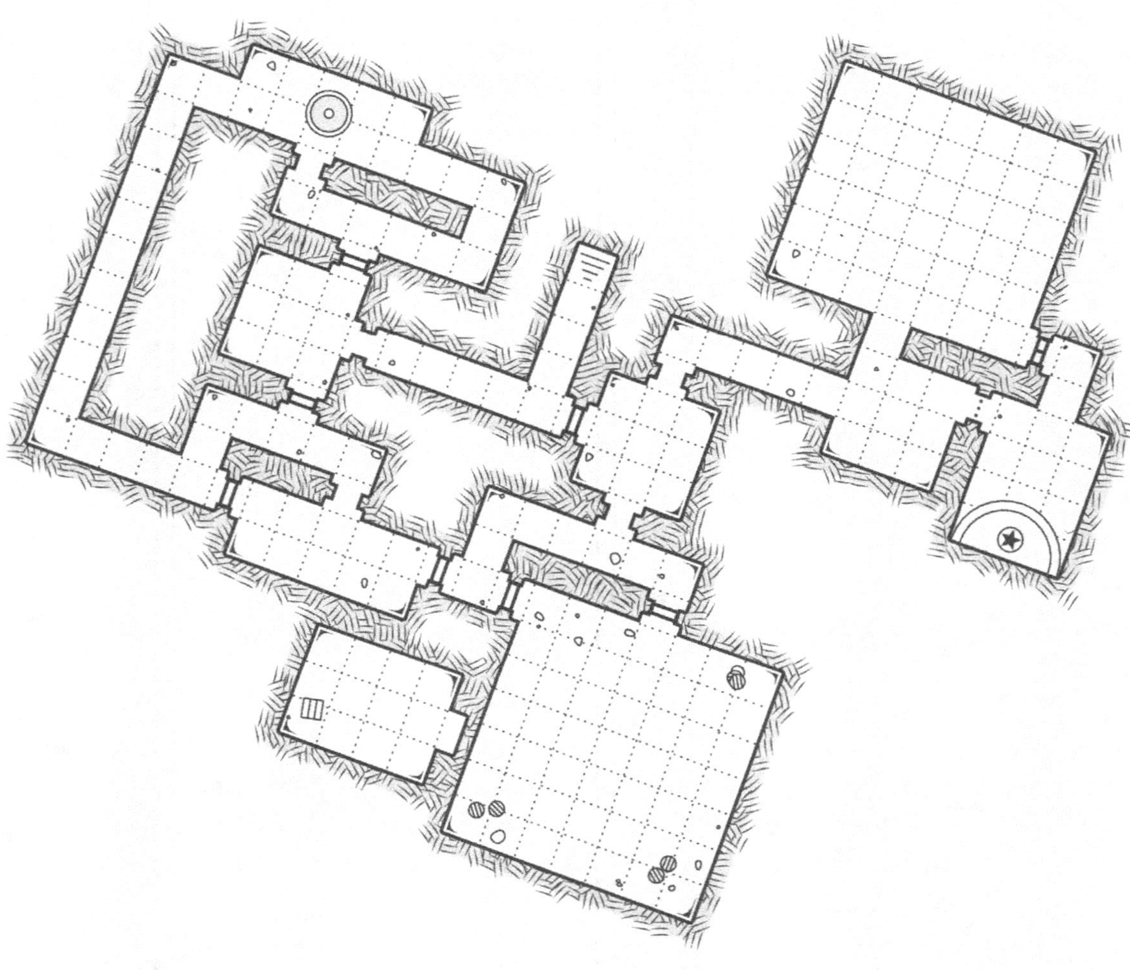

Location:

Faction:

Illumination:

Temperature:

Architecture:

Plot Hook:

History:

Inhabitants:

Points of Interest:

Upper Chambers of Terror

The chambers are situated deep in the sun-drenched dessert, far from civilization. Lately a huge man-eating boar has made its lair here. Word is that Soron, a legendary orb, is still hidden here.

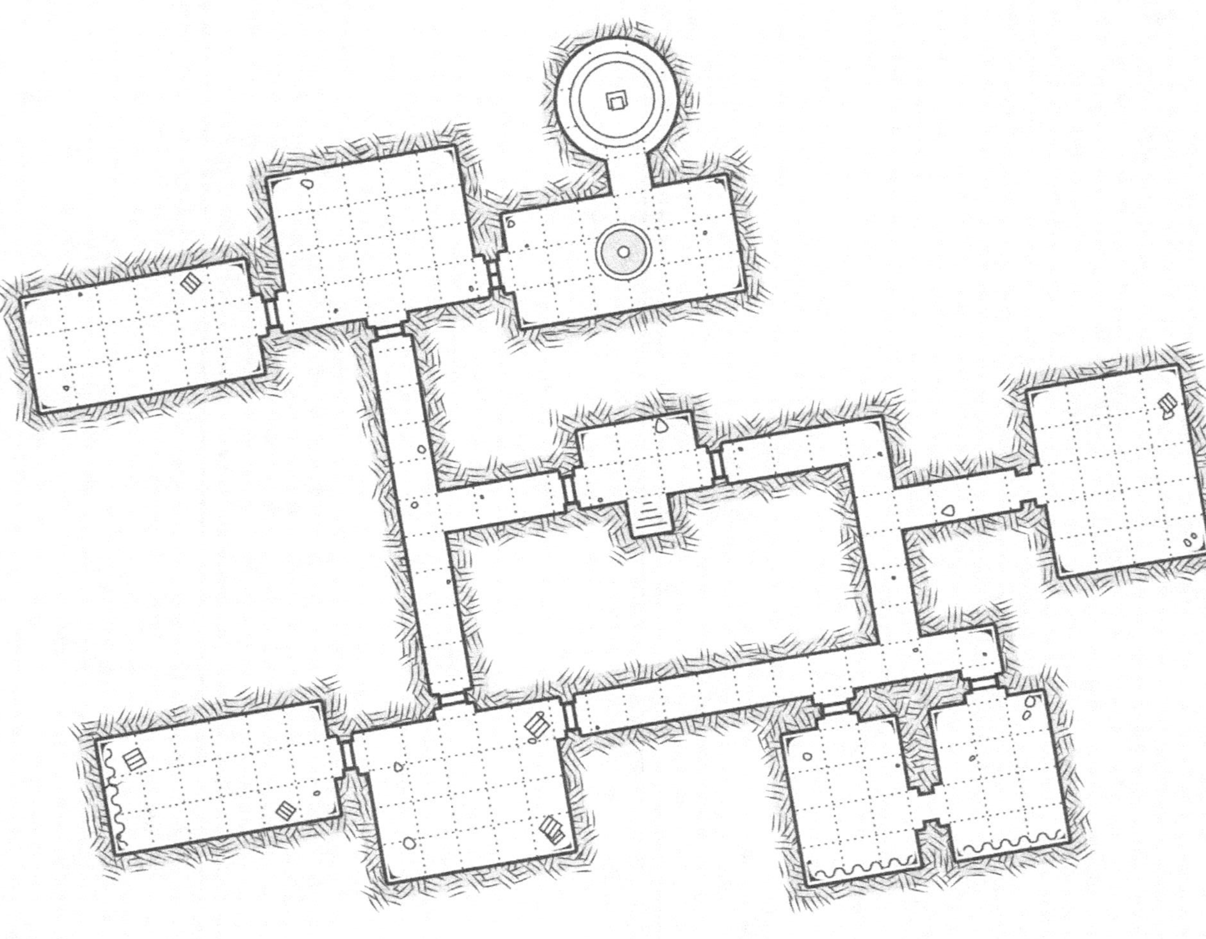

Location:	Faction:
Illumination:	Temperature:
Architecture:	
Plot Hook:	

History:

Inhabitants:

Points of Interest:

Frozen Labyrinth of Annax

For centuries the labyrinth of Annax remained sealed. Lately a terryfying dragon has made its lair here. Rumors say that Ar, a legendary tome, is still hidden here.

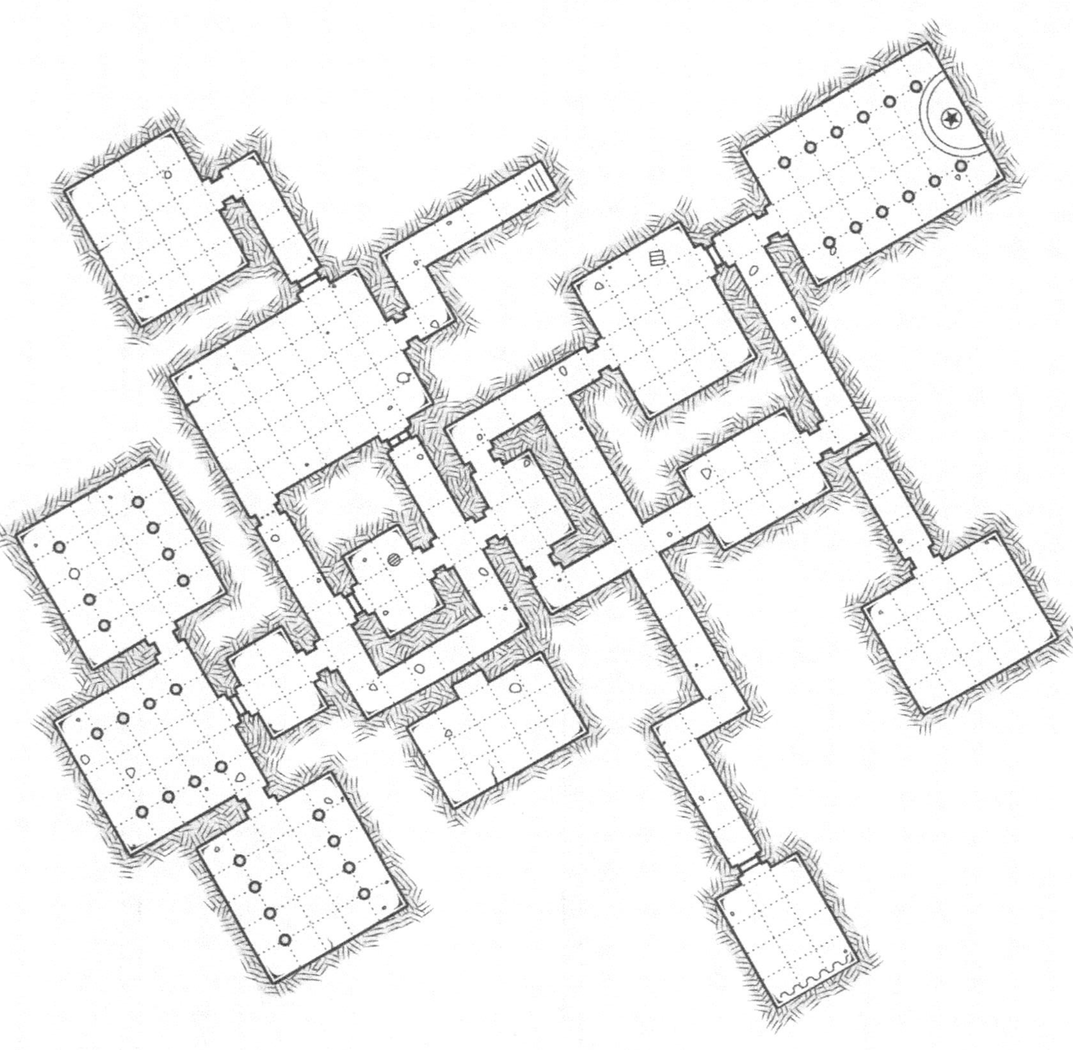

Location:

Faction:

Illumination:

Temperature:

Architecture:

Plot Hook:

History:

Inhabitants:

Points of Interest:

Nightskull Labyrinth

The labyrinth is situated deep in the marshes, in uncharted lands. Recently a party of hobgoblins rediscovered it.

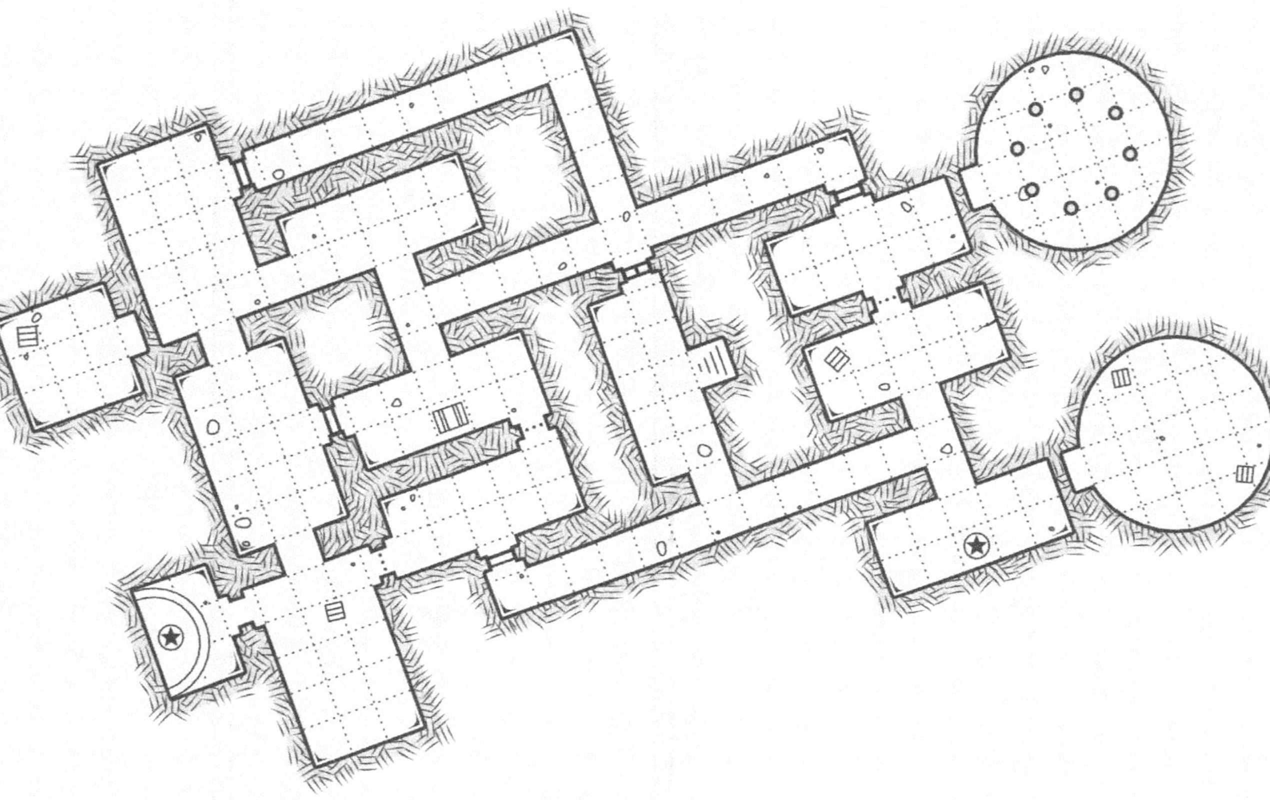

Location:	Faction:
Illumination:	Temperature:
Architecture:	
Plot Hook:	

History:

Inhabitants:

Points of Interest:

Crypt of the Cursed Beast

The crypt of the Cursed Beast is situated deep in the sun-drenched dessert, in uncharted lands. Lately it was squatted by a gang of bandits.

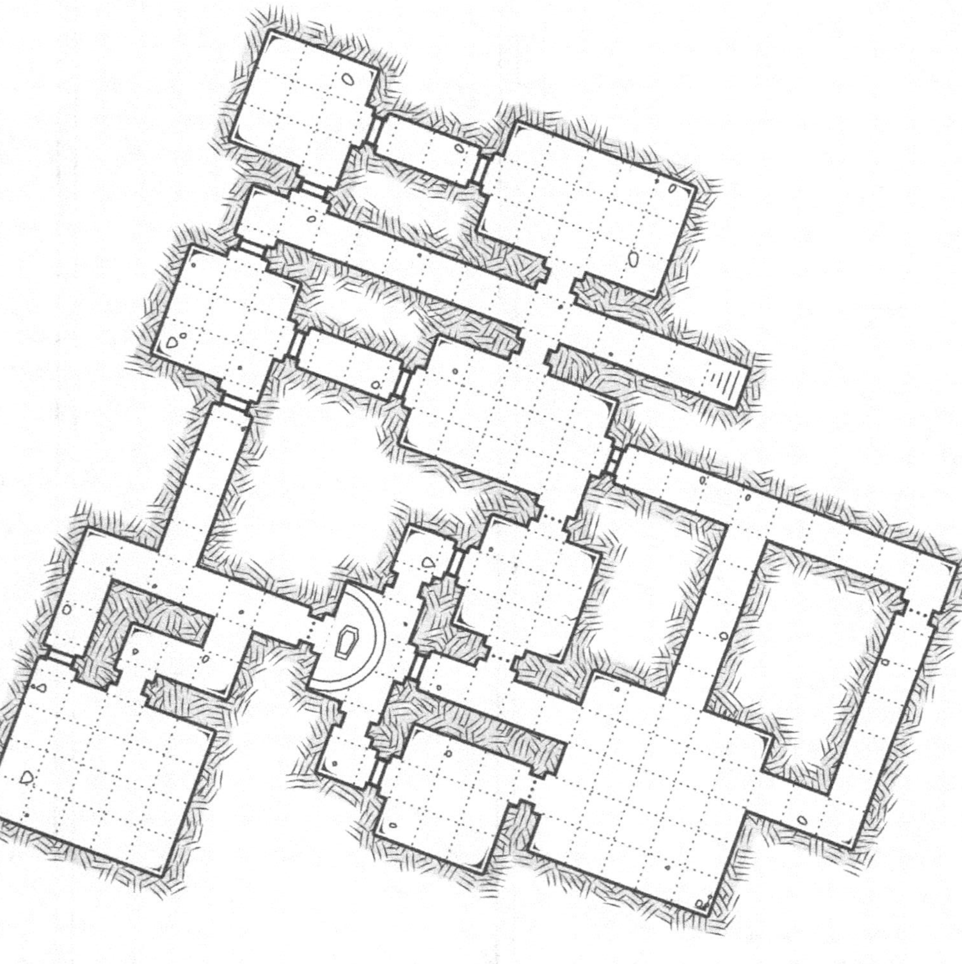

Location:	Faction:
Illumination:	Temperature:
Architecture:	
Plot Hook:	

History:

Inhabitants:

Points of Interest:

Forgotten Abbey of Evil

The abbey is situated deep in the dessert, protected by the harsh weather and dangerous local fauna. Currently it is infested by chickens, indifferent to the history of the place.

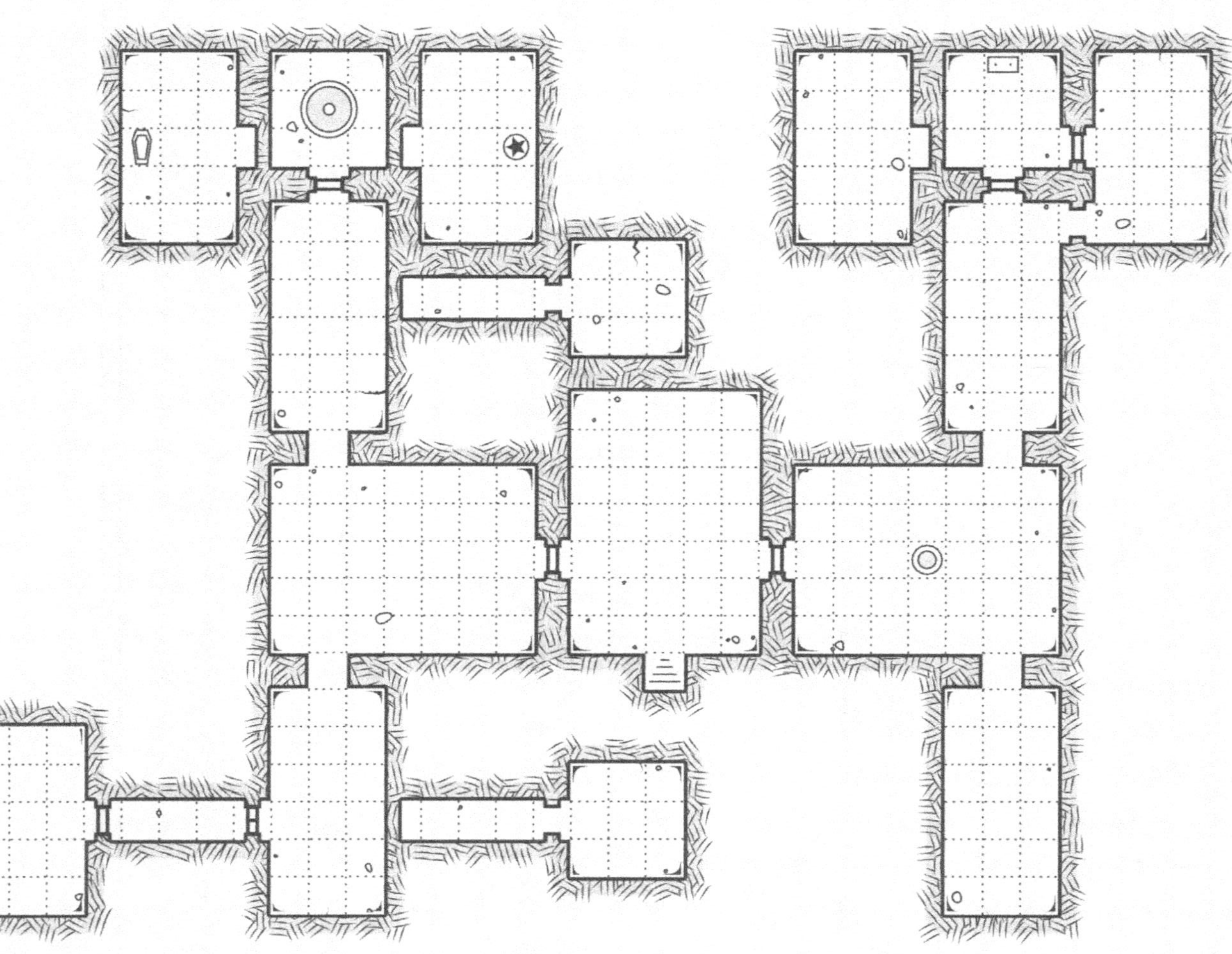

| Location: | Faction: |
| Illumination: | Temperature: |

Architecture:

Plot Hook:

History:

Inhabitants:

Points of Interest:

Library of the Vampire Priest

For a long time the library of the Vampire Priest remained sealed. Recently a party of bandits rediscovered it. It is rumored that the library is rich with treasures of magical artifacts.

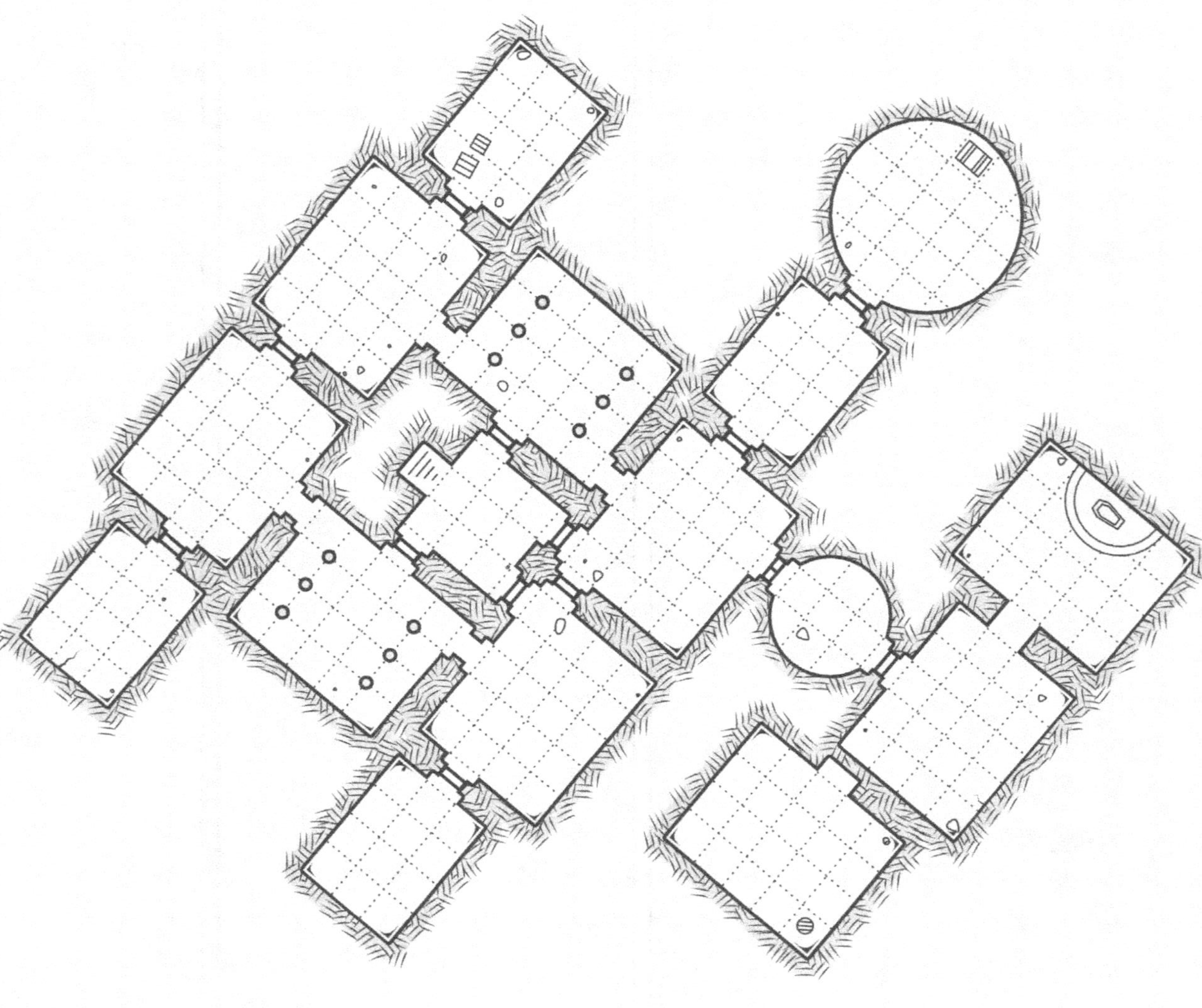

Location: Faction:

Illumination: Temperature:

Architecture:

Plot Hook:

History:

Inhabitants:

Points of Interest:

Halls of the Amber Priest

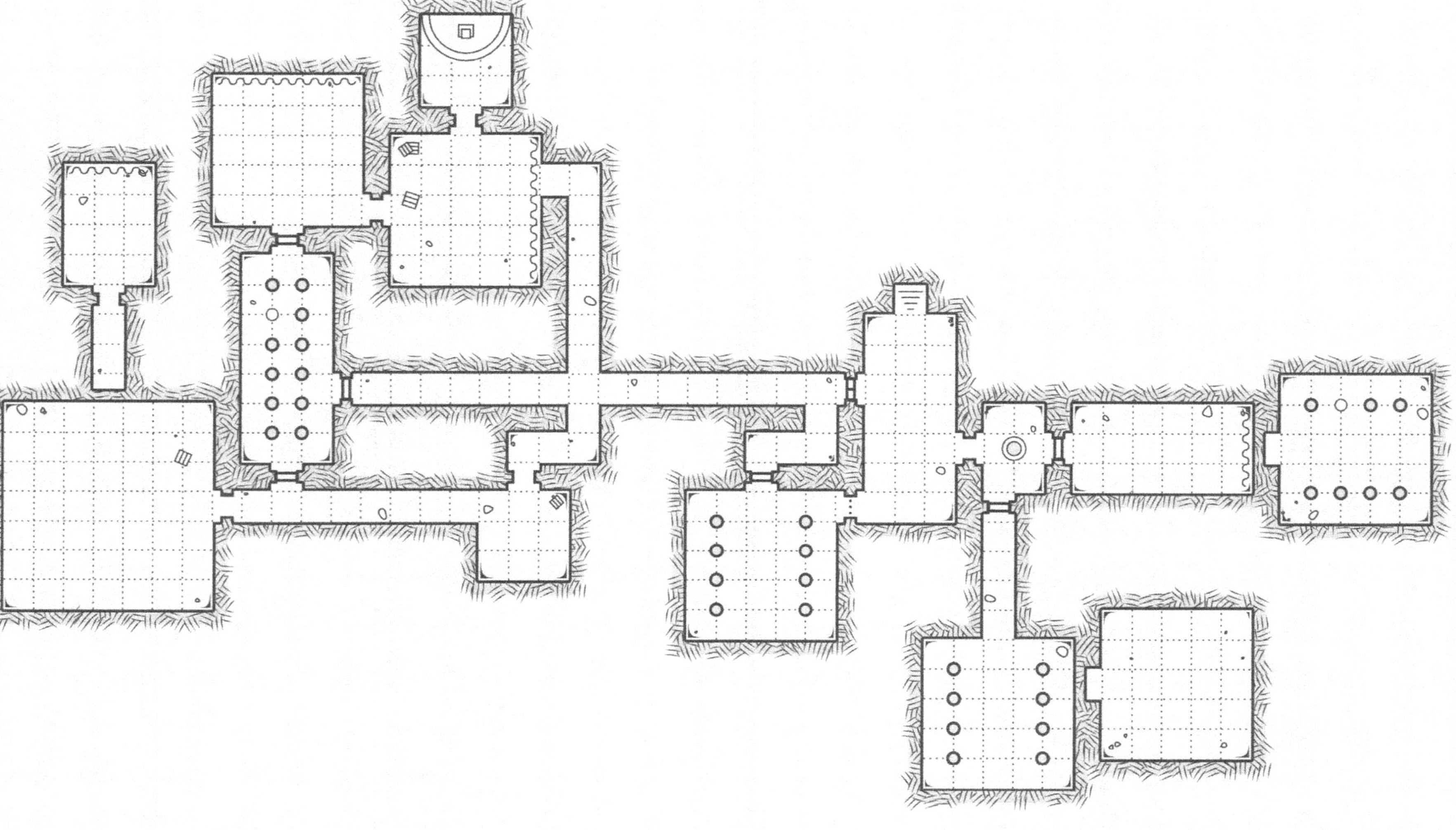

The halls of the Amber Priest are situated deep in the sun-drenched dessert, away from busy roads. These days they are badly infested by beasts. Rumors say that Kann-Zmos, a legendary lamp, is still hidden here.

Location:	Faction:
Illumination:	Temperature:
Architecture:	
Plot Hook:	

History:

Inhabitants:

Points of Interest:

Sepulcher of Mishana

For decades the sepulcher of Mishana remained uninhabited. Lately a terryfying
basilisk has made its lair here. It is rumored that Pann, a legendary orb, is hidden here.

Location:	Faction:
Illumination:	Temperature:
Architecture:	
Plot Hook:	

History:

Inhabitants:

Points of Interest:

Palace of Ice Bird

The palace is situated deep in the frozen lands, far from the nearest town. Lately a huge man-eating boar has made its lair here. The palace is a place of growth of a rare specie of mushrooms.

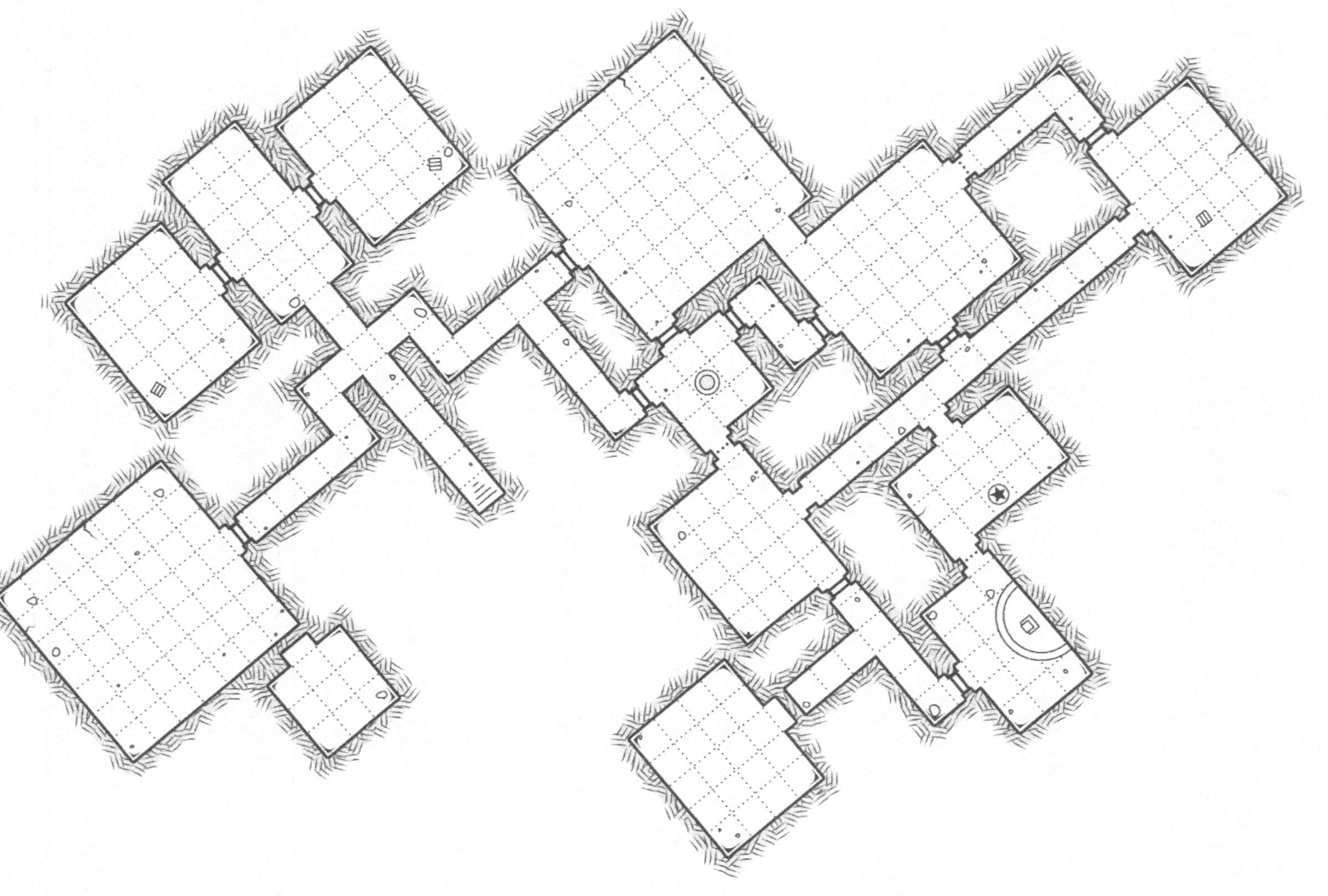

| Location: | Faction: |
| Illumination: | Temperature: |

Architecture:

Plot Hook:

History:

Inhabitants:

Points of Interest:

Twilight Castle of the Vampire Lady

After being destroyed by a great fire decades ago the castle of the Vampire Lady remained uninhabited.
Recently a giant man-eating crow has made its lair here. It is rumored that Kos, a legendary doll, is hidden here.

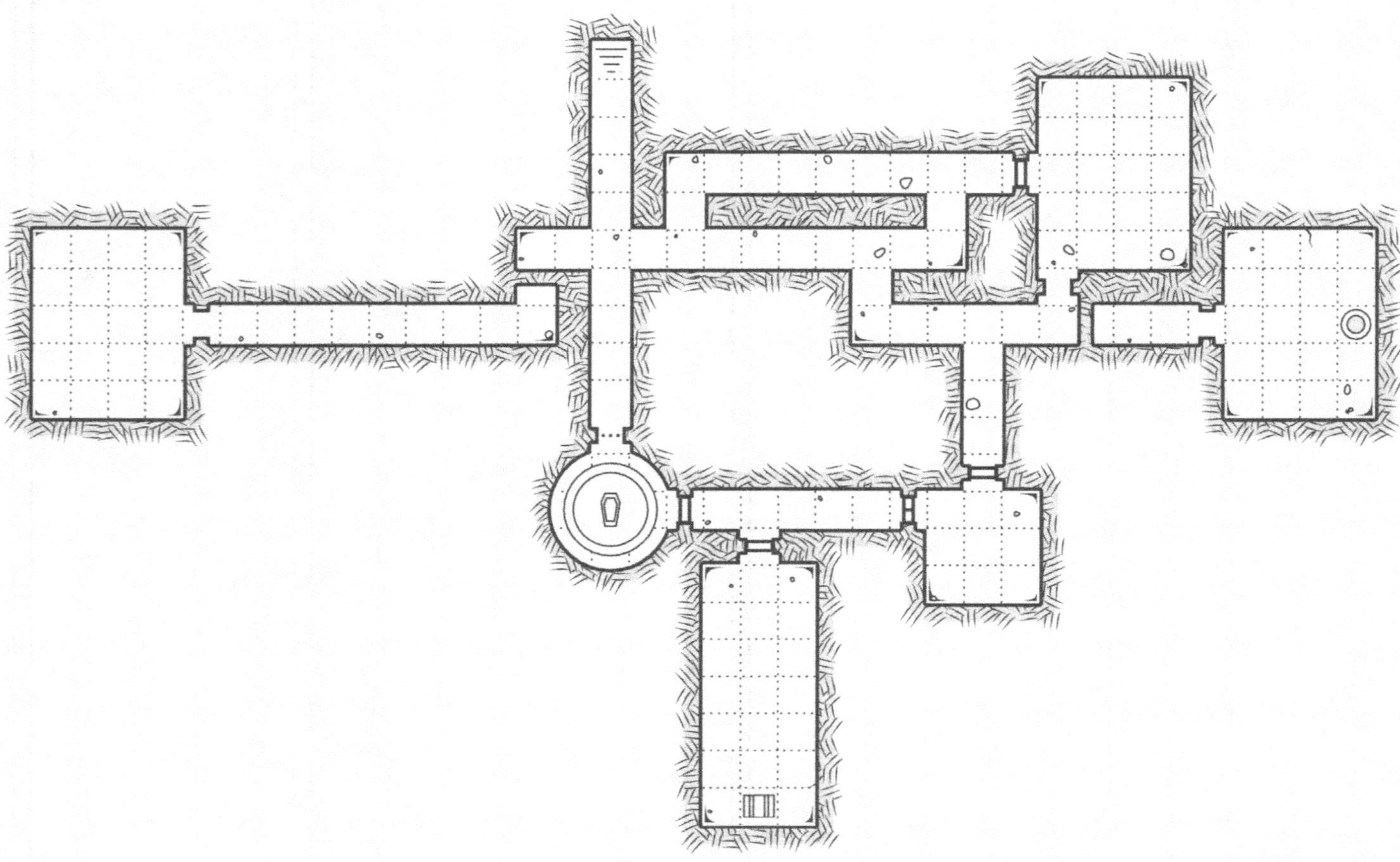

Location:	Faction:
Illumination:	Temperature:
Architecture:	
Plot Hook:	

History:

Inhabitants:

Points of Interest:

Forbidden Catacombs of the Iron Lady

After being destroyed by a horrible magic storm decades ago the catacombs of the Iron Lady remained abandoned. Lately a party of hobgoblins rediscovered they, making they their center of operation. Rumors say that the catacombs are rich with treasures of gold.

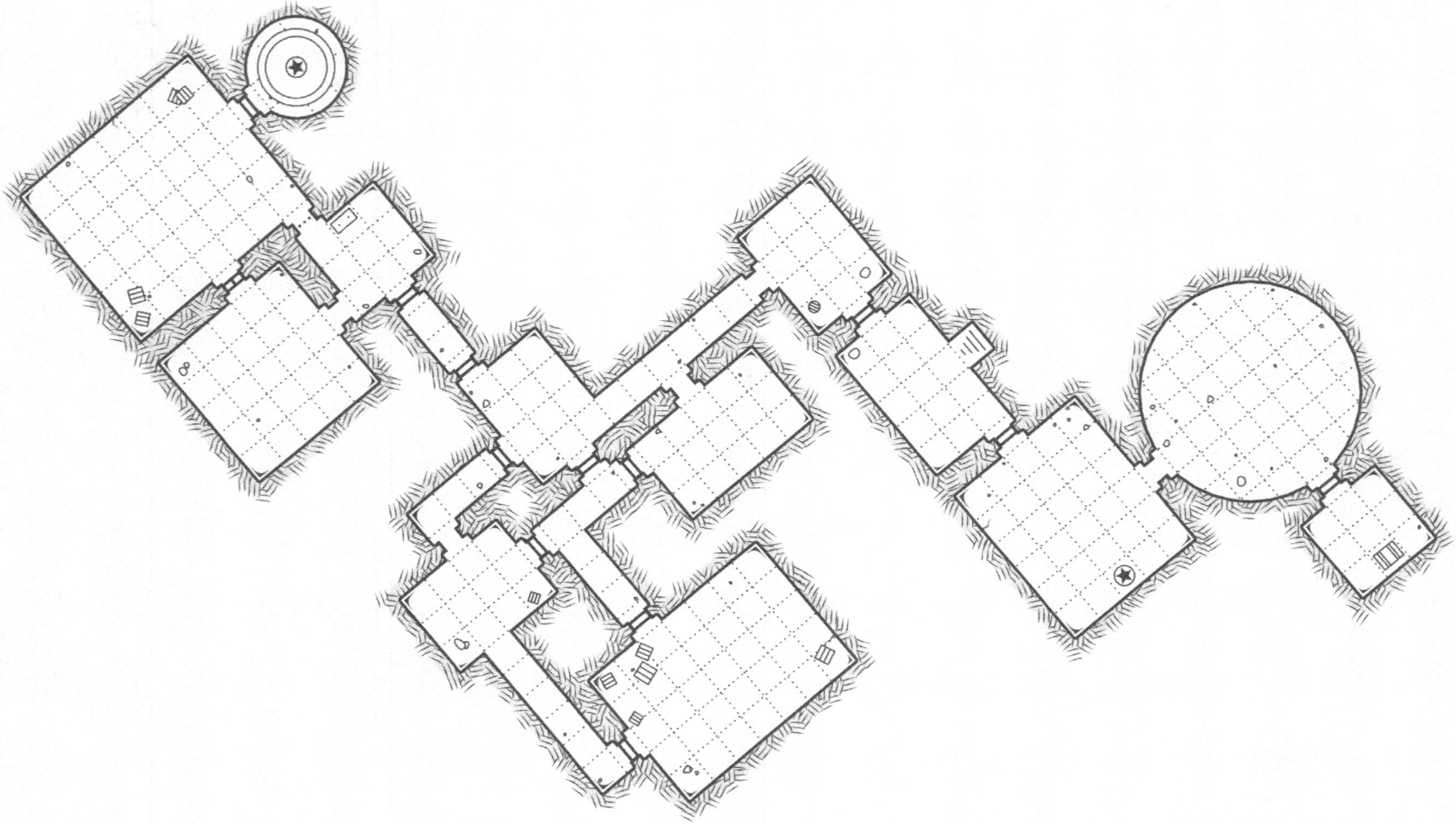

<table>
<tr><td>Location:</td><td>Faction:</td></tr>
<tr><td>Illumination:</td><td>Temperature:</td></tr>
<tr><td colspan="2">Architecture:</td></tr>
<tr><td colspan="2">Plot Hook:</td></tr>
</table>

History:

Inhabitants:

Points of Interest:

Archive of the Cursed Knight

The archive of the Cursed Knight is situated deep in the marshes, away from busy roads. Recently a huge man-eating sparrow has made its lair here.

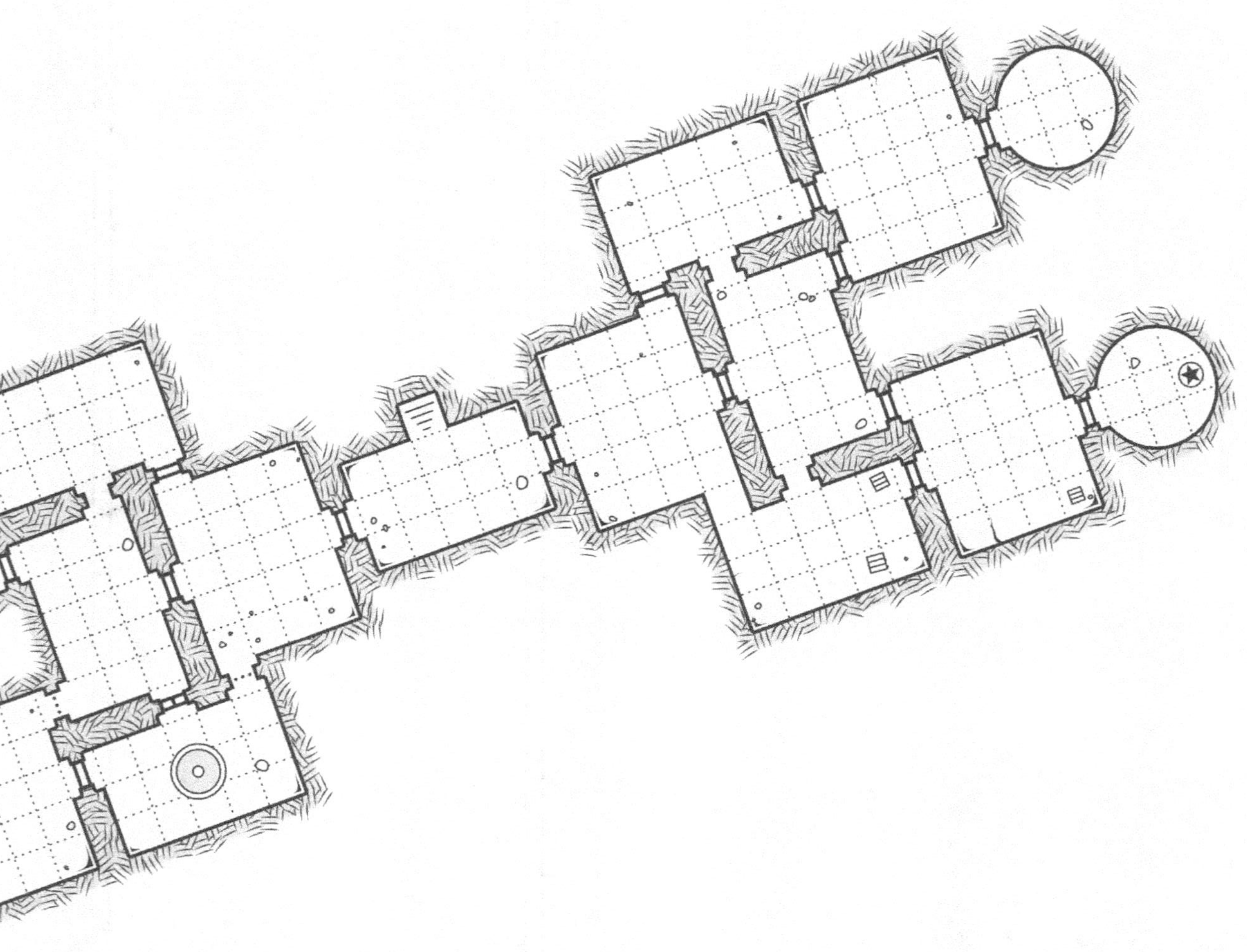

Location: Faction:

Illumination: Temperature:

Architecture:

Plot Hook:

History:

Inhabitants:

Points of Interest:

Palace of Blades

For a long time the palace remained sealed. Currently it is badly infested by pigs, which don't care about the history of the place. The palace is a place of growth of a valuable specie of fungi.

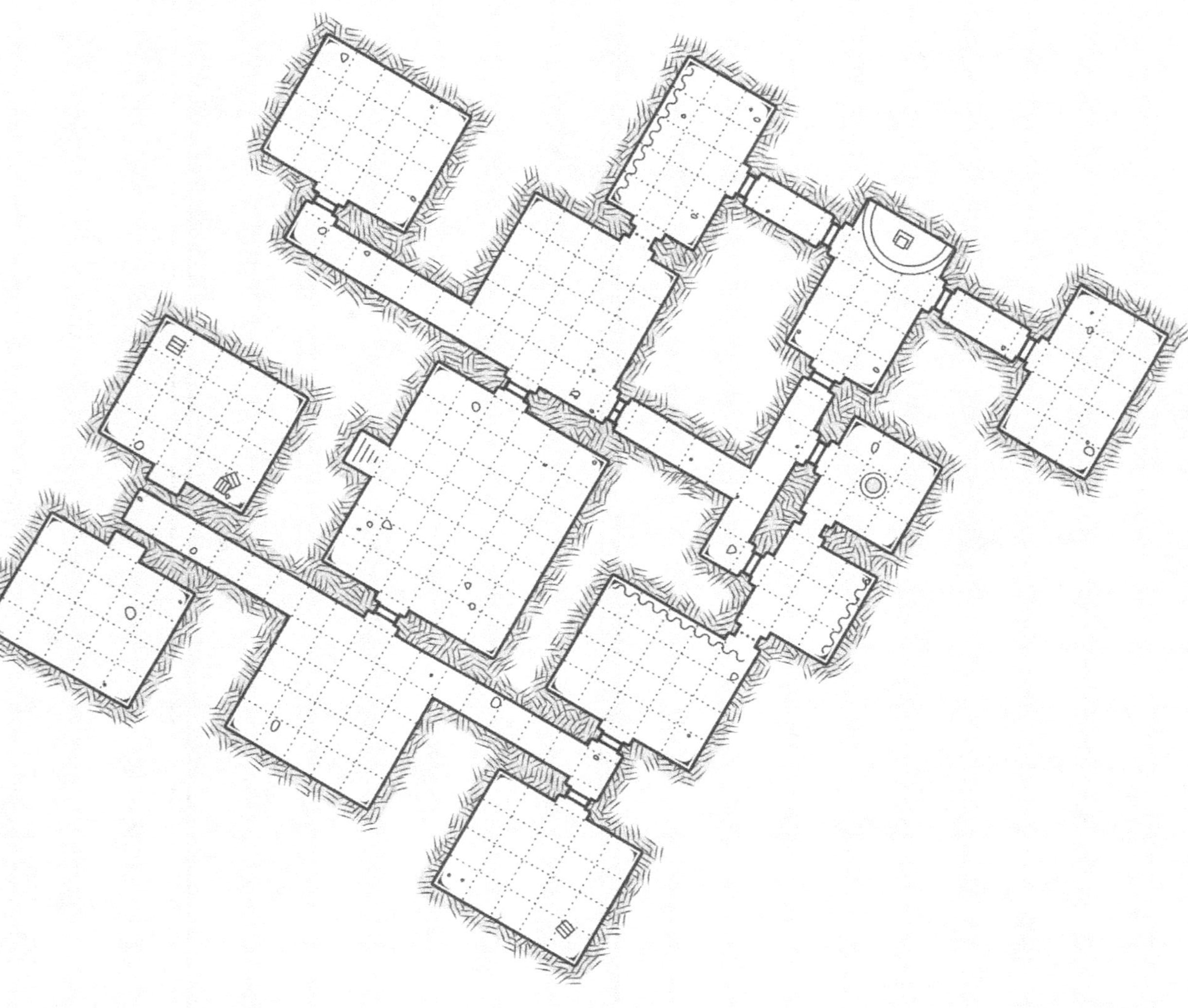

Location: Faction:

Illumination: Temperature:

Architecture:

Plot Hook:

History:

Inhabitants:

Points of Interest:

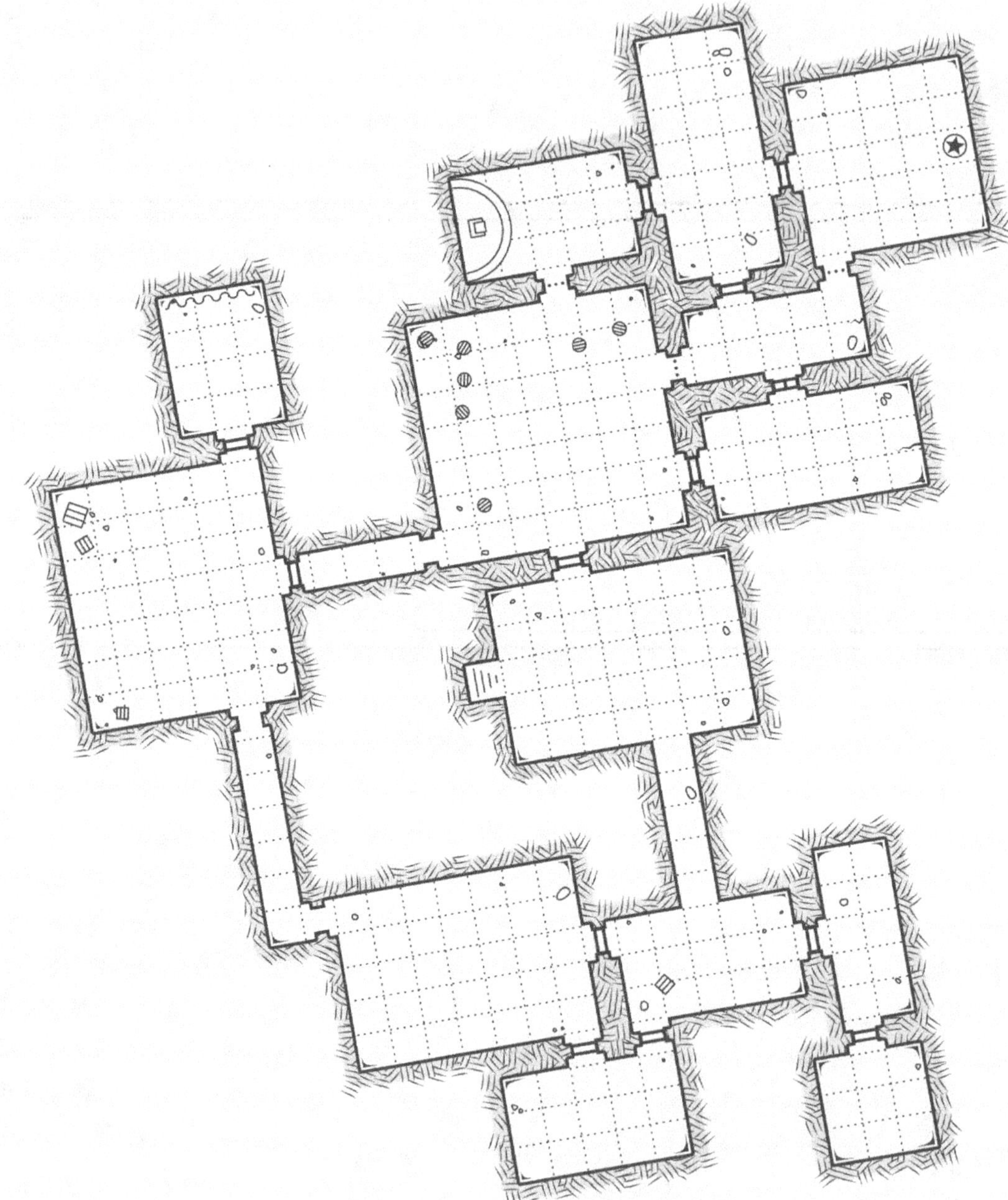

Forgotten Halls of Plague Arrow

The halls are situated deep in the high mountains, protected by the impassable terrain and dangerous local fauna. Currently they are badly infested by boars.

Location:	Faction:
Illumination:	Temperature:
Architecture:	
Plot Hook:	

History:

Inhabitants:

Points of Interest:

Twilight Temple of Skava

For many years the temple of Skava remained uninhabited. These days it is infested by sparrows.

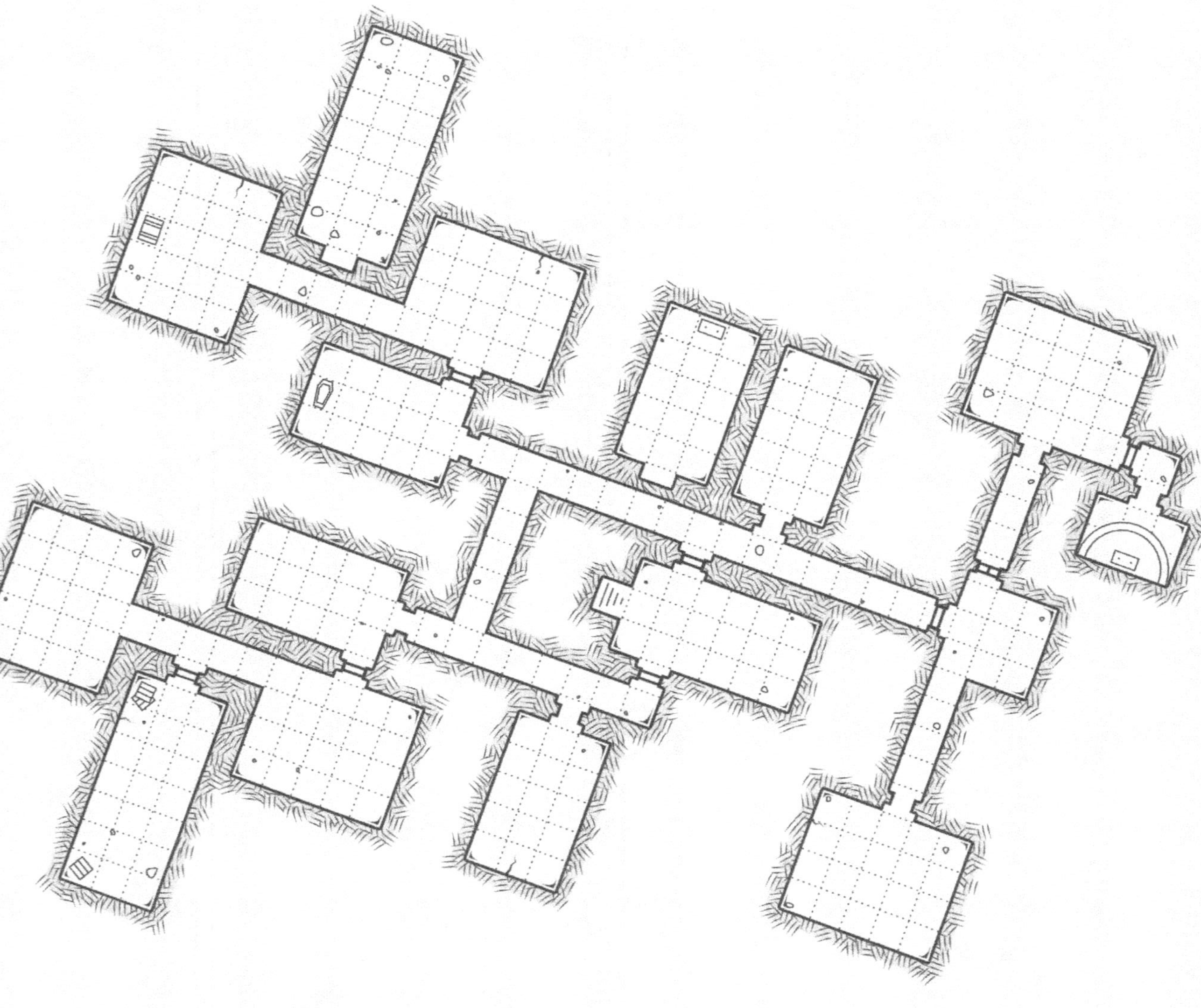

Location:	Faction:
Illumination:	Temperature:
Architecture:	
Plot Hook:	

History:

Inhabitants:

Points of Interest:

Subterranean Monastery of Barinna

*The monastery of Barinna is situated deep in the jungle, far
from the nearest town. Lately it was squatted by a band of orcs.*

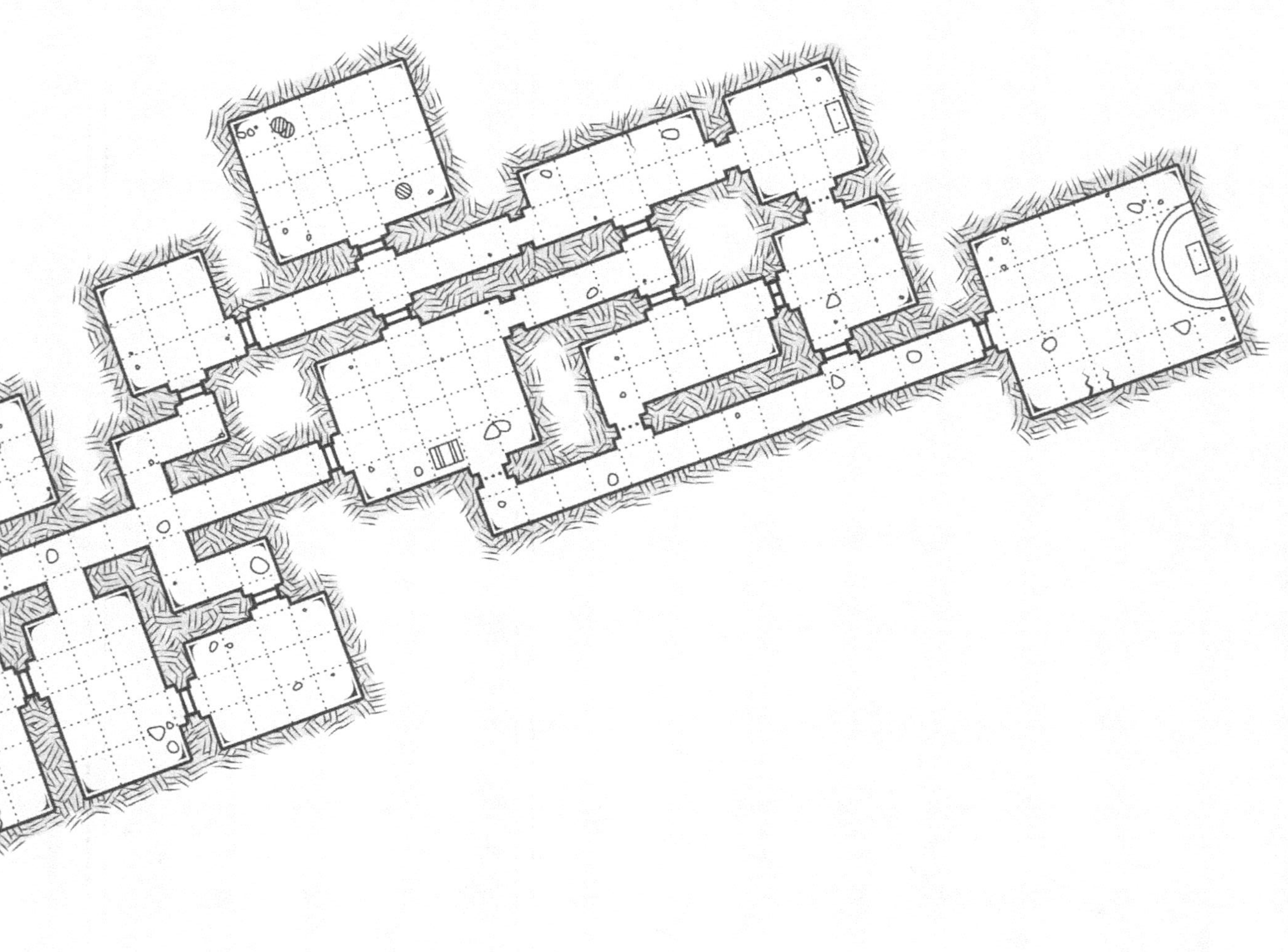

Location:	Faction:
Illumination:	Temperature:
Architecture:	
Plot Hook:	

History:

Inhabitants:

Points of Interest:

Grimspear Prison

The prison is situated deep in the dessert, protected by the dangerous local fauna and harsh weather. These days it is infested by pigs. Word is that Kar, a legendary compass, is still hidden here.

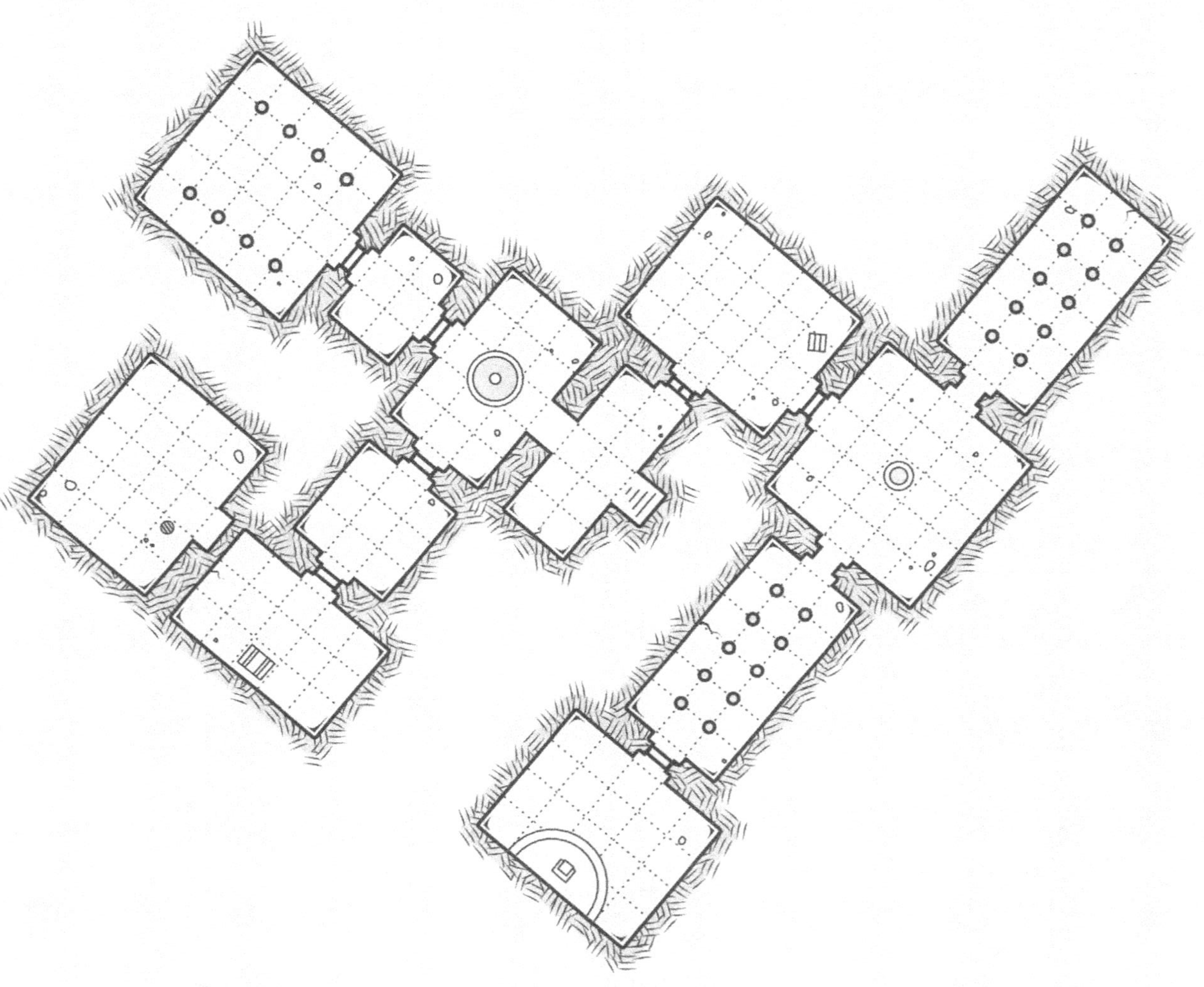

Location:	Faction:
Illumination:	Temperature:

Architecture:

Plot Hook:

History:

Inhabitants:

Points of Interest:

Subterranean Maze of Perai

The maze of Perai is situated deep in the swamps, far from civilization. Currently it is infested by pigs. Word is that Tyron, a legendary staff, is hidden here.

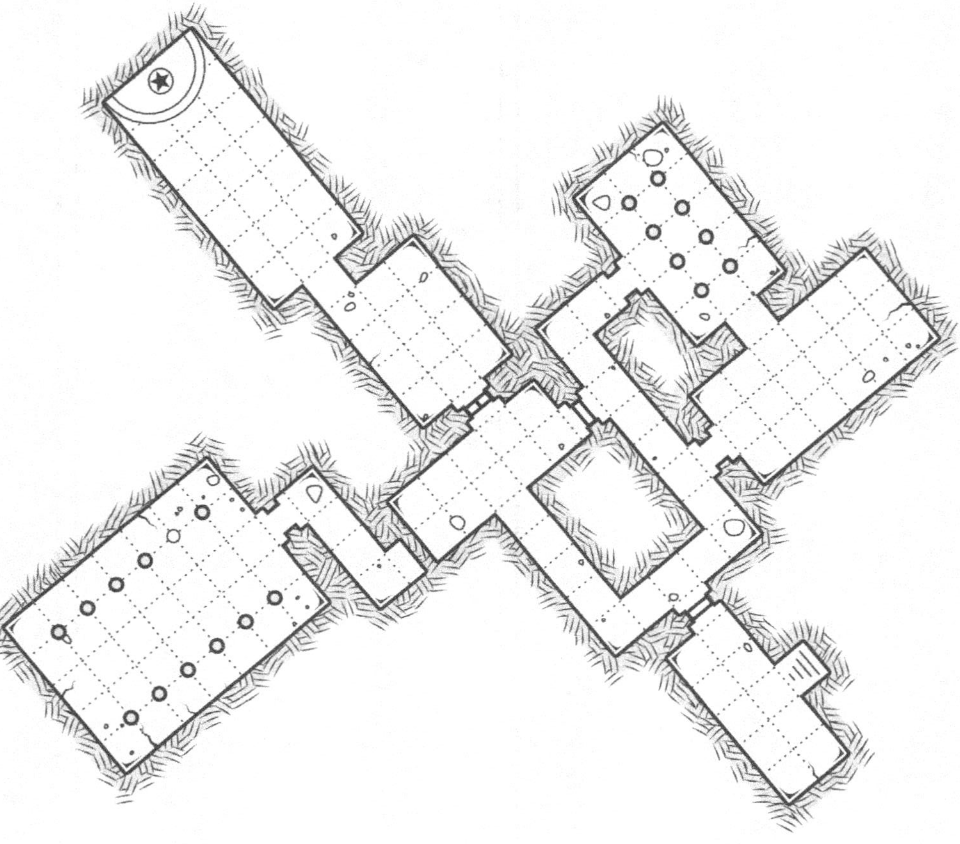

Location:	Faction:
Illumination:	Temperature:

Architecture:

Plot Hook:

History:

Inhabitants:

Points of Interest:

Veiled Archive of the Cursed Knight

After being destroyed by a terrible storm decades ago the archive of the Cursed Knight remained deserted. Recently a gang of cultists rediscovered it, making it their center of operation.

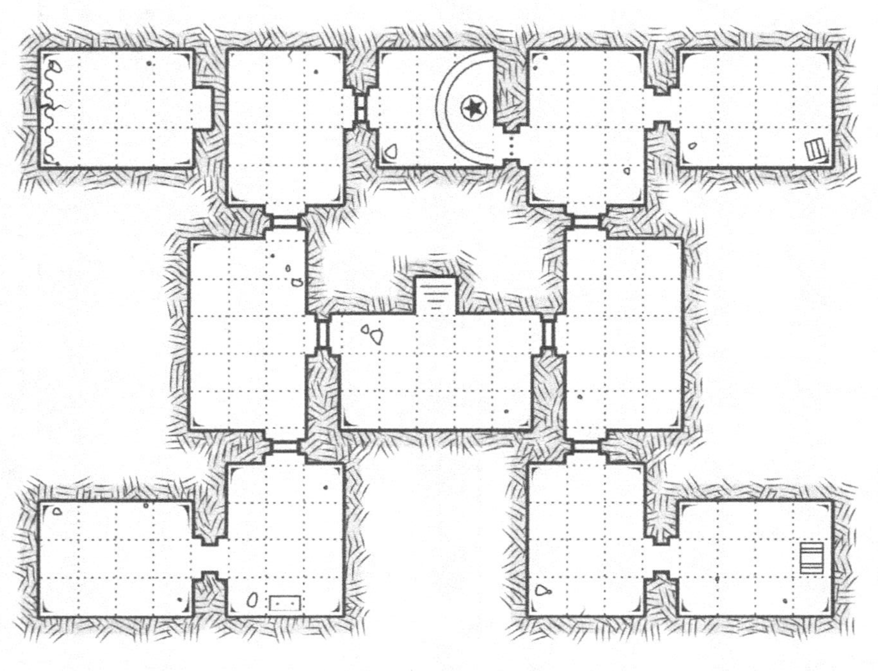

Location:	Faction:
Illumination:	Temperature:
Architecture:	
Plot Hook:	

History:

Inhabitants:

Points of Interest:

Frozen Catacombs of Kari

The catacombs of Kari are situated deep in the frozen lands, protected by the impassable terrain.
Currently they are infested by mammoths, which don't care about the history of the place.

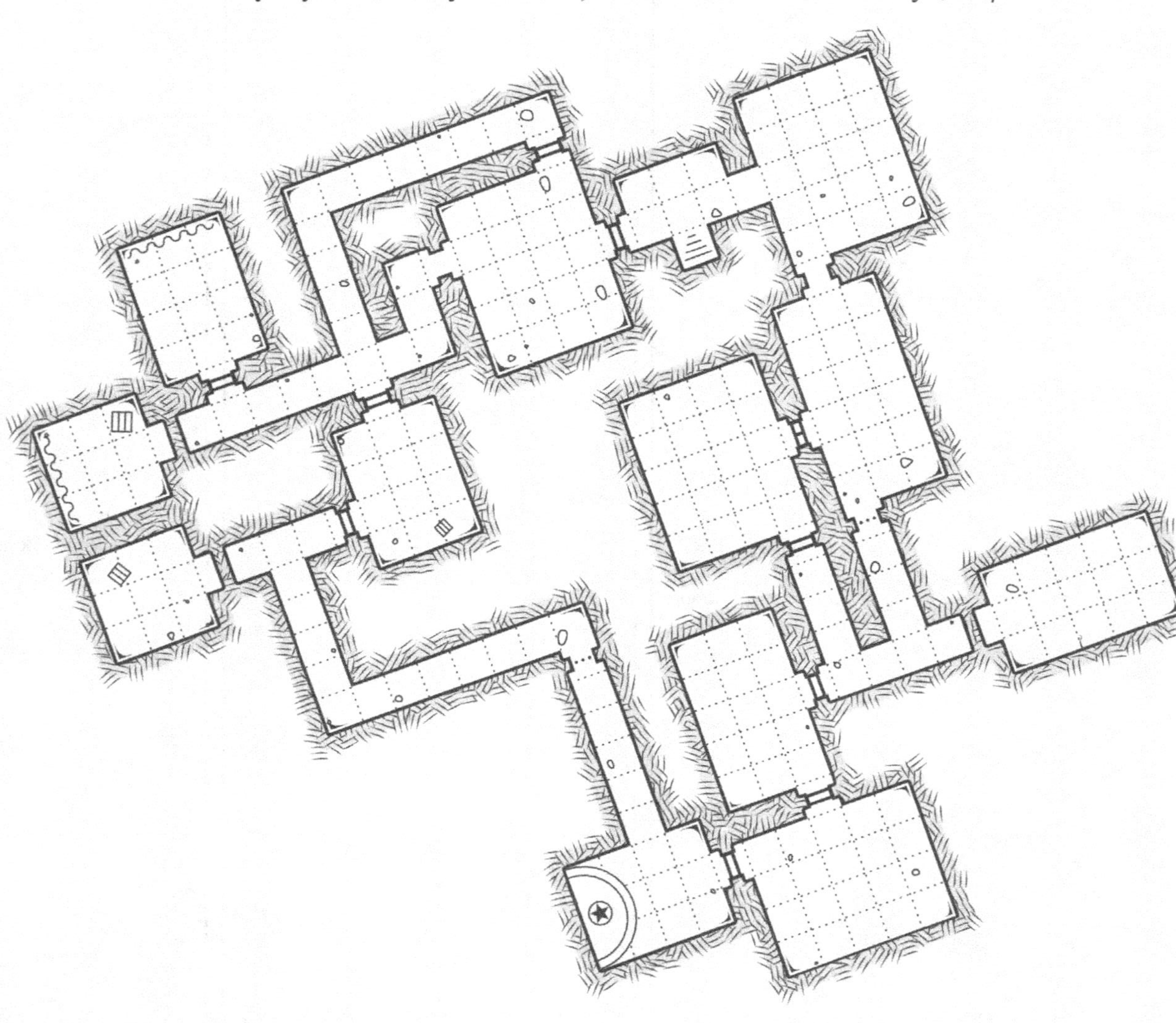

Location: Faction:

Illumination: Temperature:

Architecture:

Plot Hook:

History:

Inhabitants:

Points of Interest:

Monastery of the Leper Baron

For a long time the monastery of the Leper Baron remained sealed. Lately it was squatted by a party of bandits.

Location:	Faction:
Illumination:	Temperature:
Architecture:	
Plot Hook:	

History:

Inhabitants:

Points of Interest:

Underwater Maze of the Red Prince

For many years the maze of the Red Prince remained sealed. Lately a giant venomous ant has made its home here.

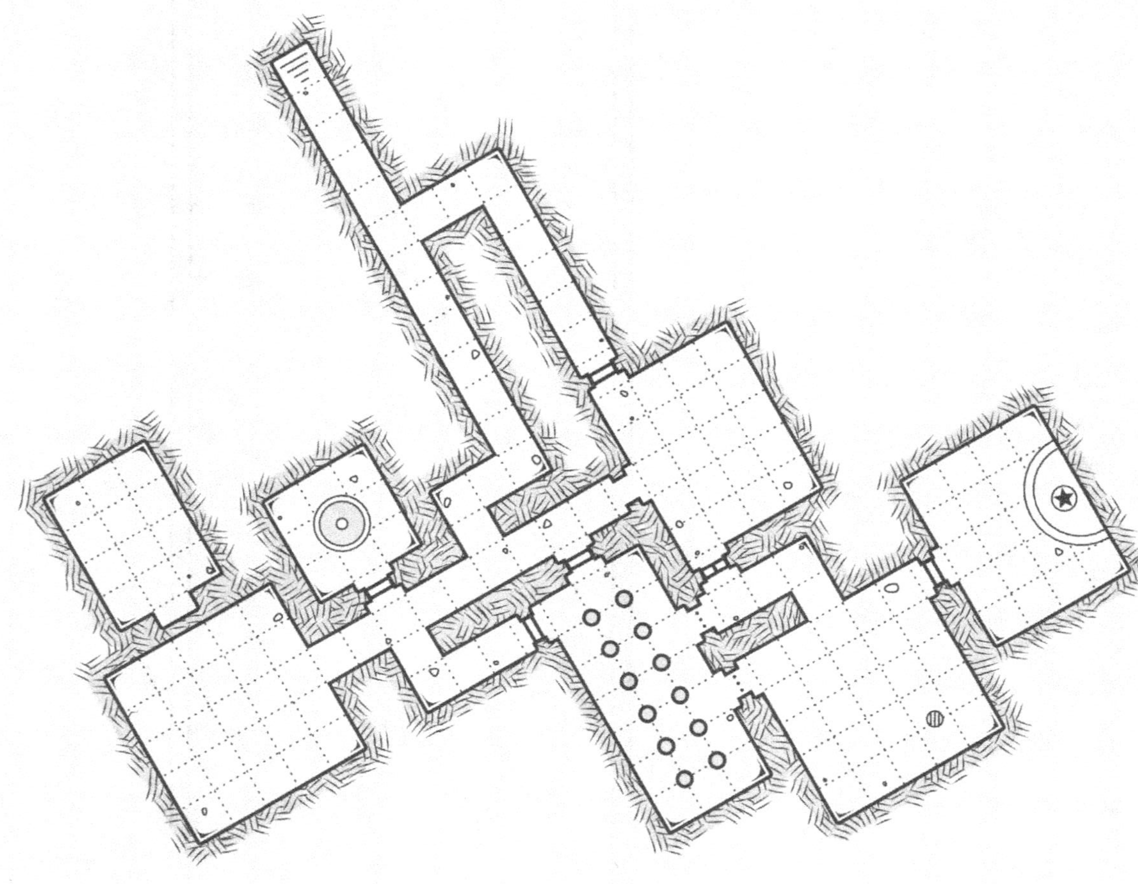

Location: Faction:

Illumination: Temperature:

Architecture:

Plot Hook:

History:

Inhabitants:

Points of Interest:

Monastery of Frost Bird

After being destroyed by a great storm a long time ago the monastery remained deserted. Recently a giant mutant lizard has made its home here. Word is that the monastery is rich with treasures of gold and magical artifacts.

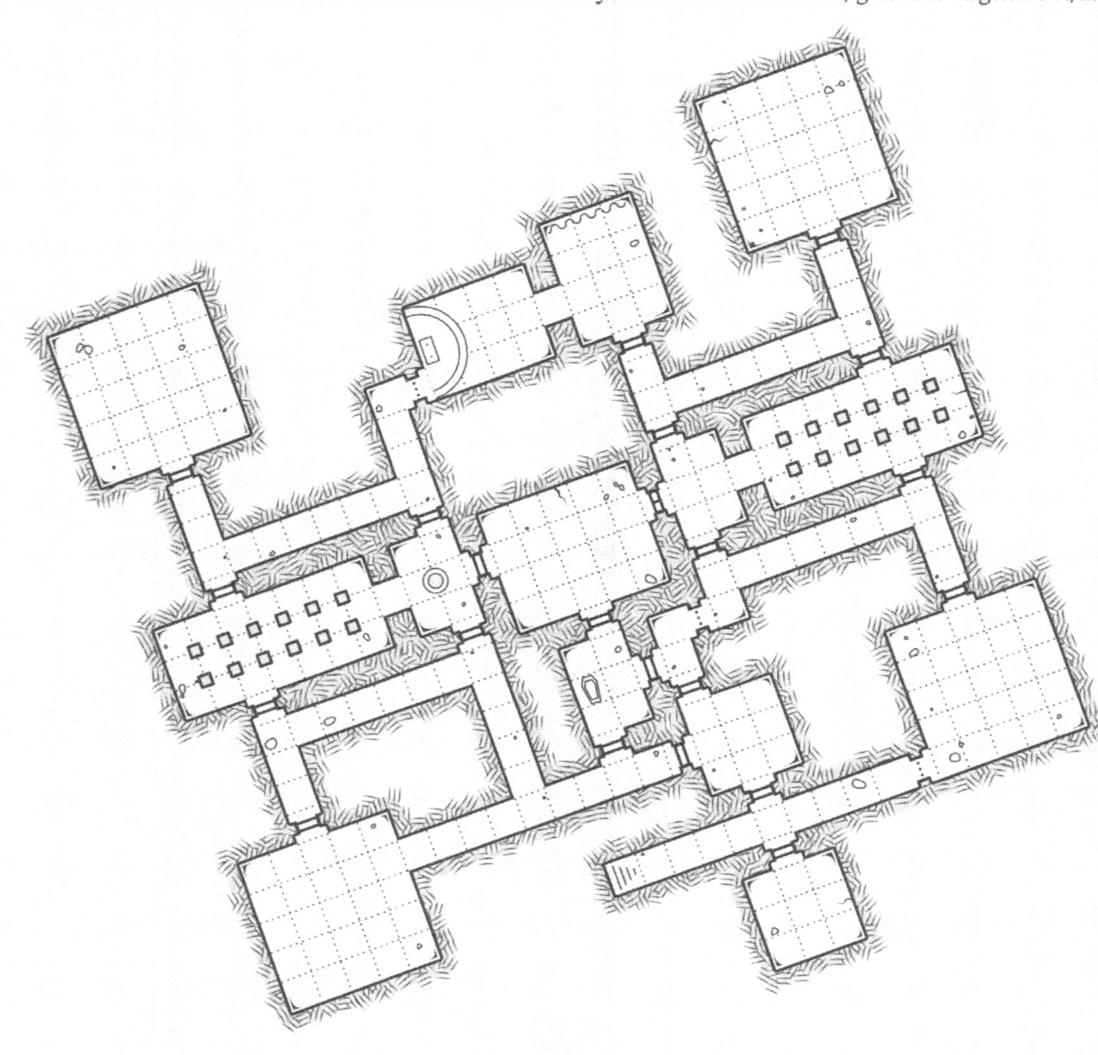

Location:	Faction:
Illumination:	Temperature:
Architecture:	
Plot Hook:	

History:

Inhabitants:

Points of Interest:

Monastery of the Viper Prince

The monastery of the Viper Prince is situated deep in the high mountains, away from busy roads. These days it is infested by beasts. The monastery of the Viper Prince is home to a highly valued specie of fungi.

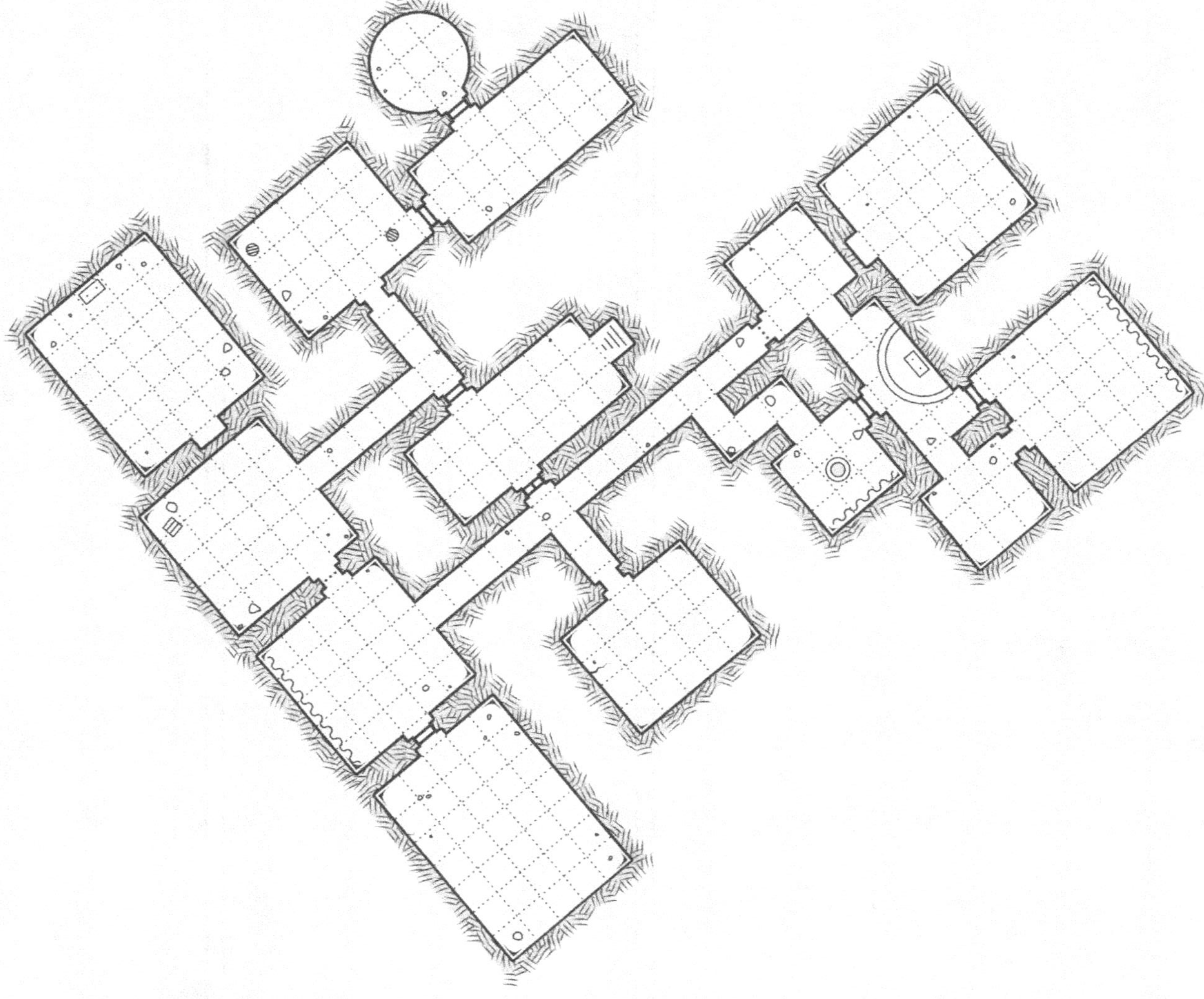

Location: Faction:

Illumination: Temperature:

Architecture:

Plot Hook:

History:

Inhabitants:

Points of Interest:

Frozen Vault of Orva

For a long time the vault of Orva was considered lost. Recently an undead basilisk has made its lair here. The vault of Orva is home to a rare specie of herbs.

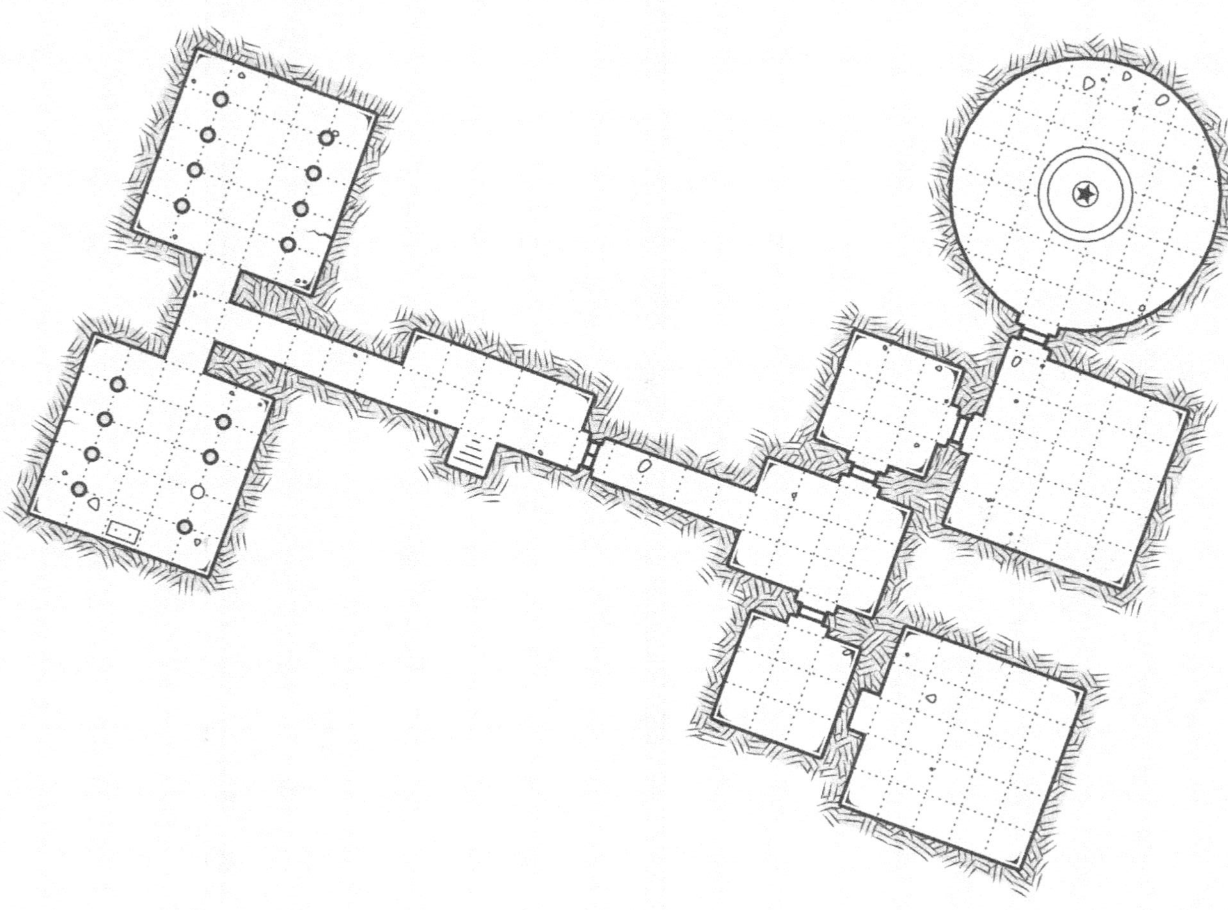

Location:	Faction:
Illumination:	Temperature:
Architecture:	
Plot Hook:	

History:

Inhabitants:

Points of Interest:

Infected Palace of the Diamond Beast

After being destroyed by a great magic storm a long time ago the palace of the Diamond Beast remained uninhabited. These days it is infested by wolfs. The palace of the Diamond Beast is a place of growth of a rare specie of herbs.

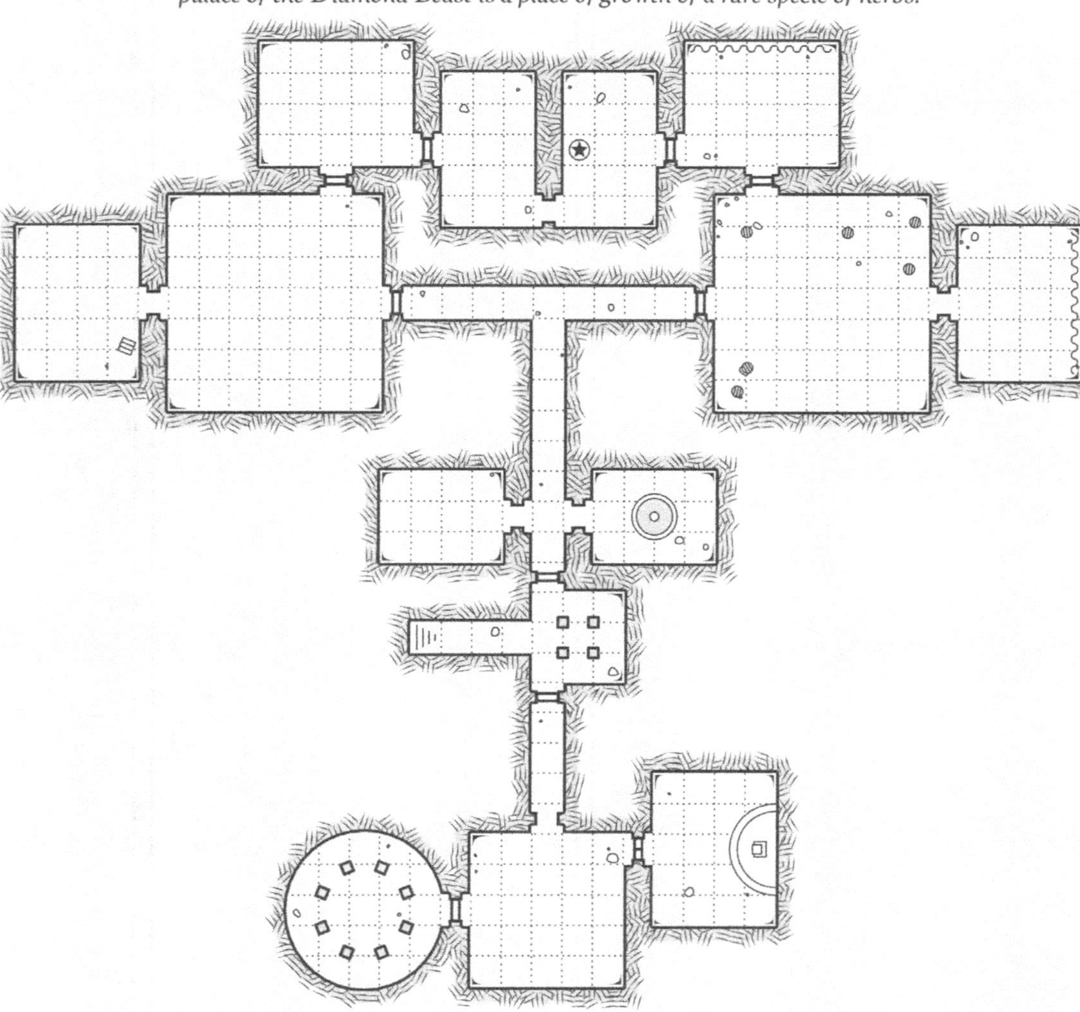

Location:	Faction:
Illumination:	Temperature:
Architecture:	
Plot Hook:	

History:

Inhabitants:

Points of Interest:

Monastery of the Great Messiah

The monastery of the Great Messiah is situated deep in the mountains, in uncharted lands. Recently a gang of pirates rediscovered it, making it their center of operation. The monastery of the Great Messiah is a place of growth of a valuable specie of fungi.

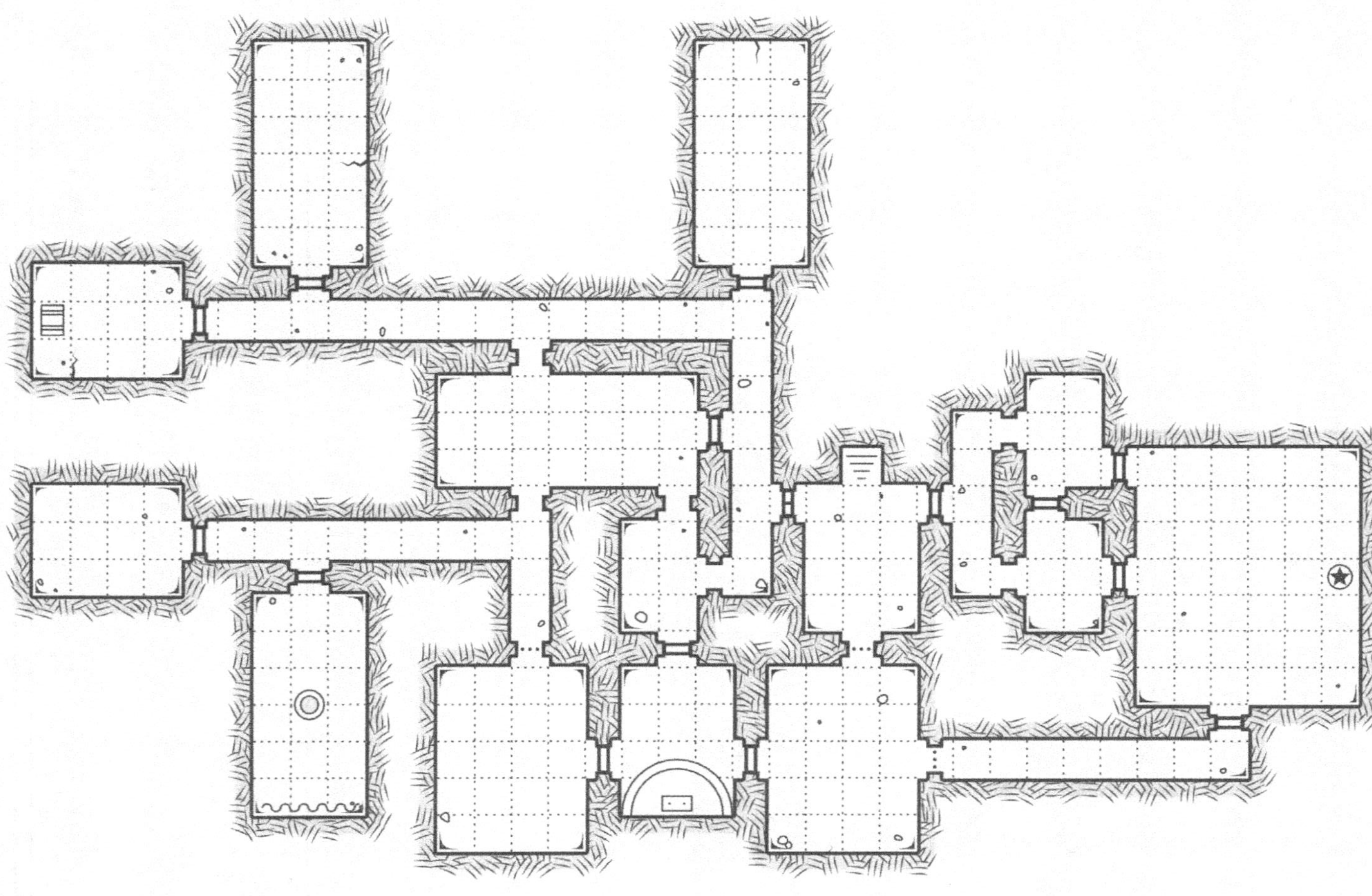

Location: Faction:

Illumination: Temperature:

Architecture:

Plot Hook:

History:

Inhabitants:

Points of Interest:

Veiled Labyrinth of the Storm Witch

The Storm Witch is long dead, but people are still reluctant to come close to the labyrinth.
These days it is badly infested by bats, which don't care about the history of the place.

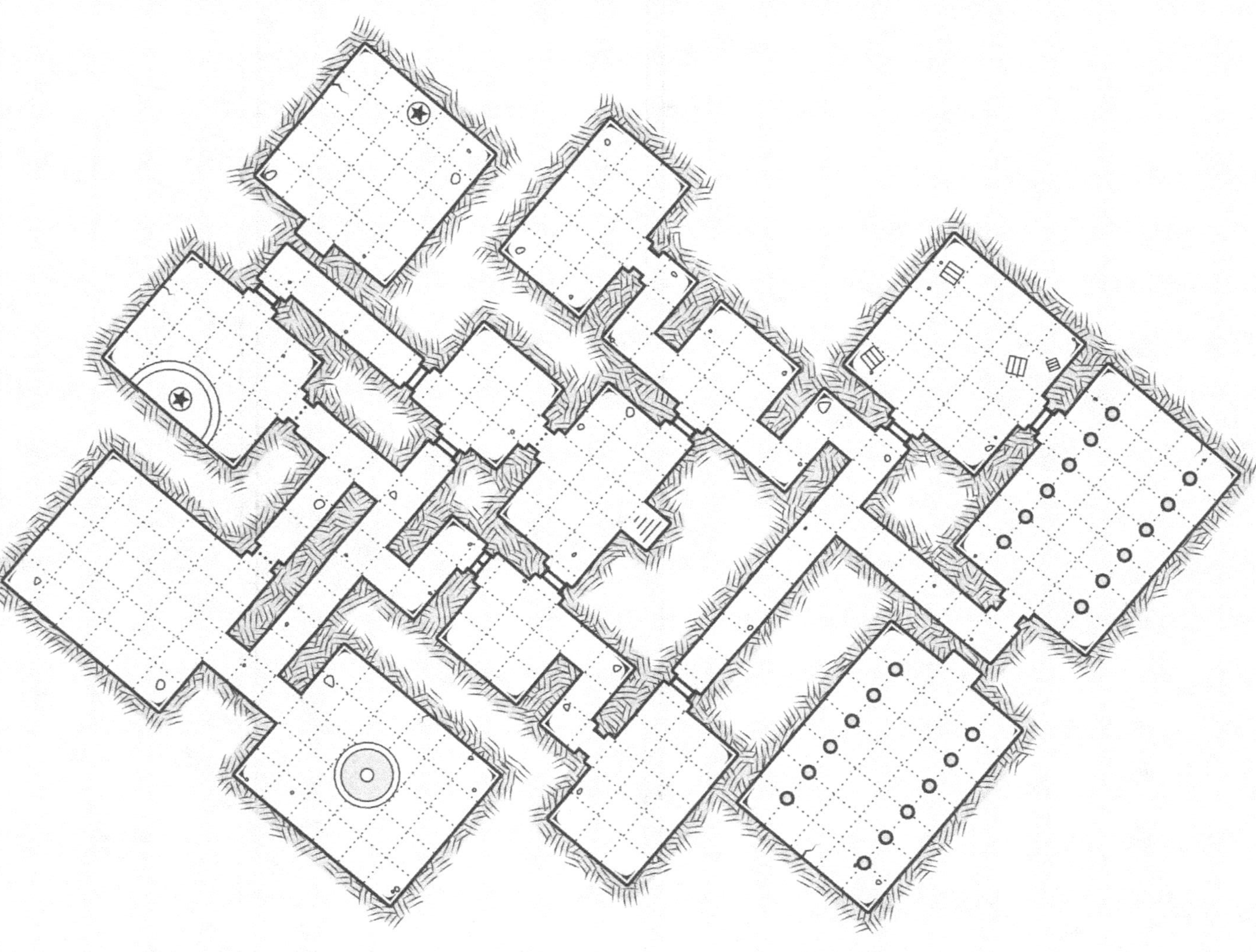

Location:	Faction:
Illumination:	Temperature:
Architecture:	
Plot Hook:	

History:

Inhabitants:

Points of Interest:

Haunted Mansion of Illusions

For many years the mansion was considered lost. These days it is infested by lizards, which don't care about the history of the place.

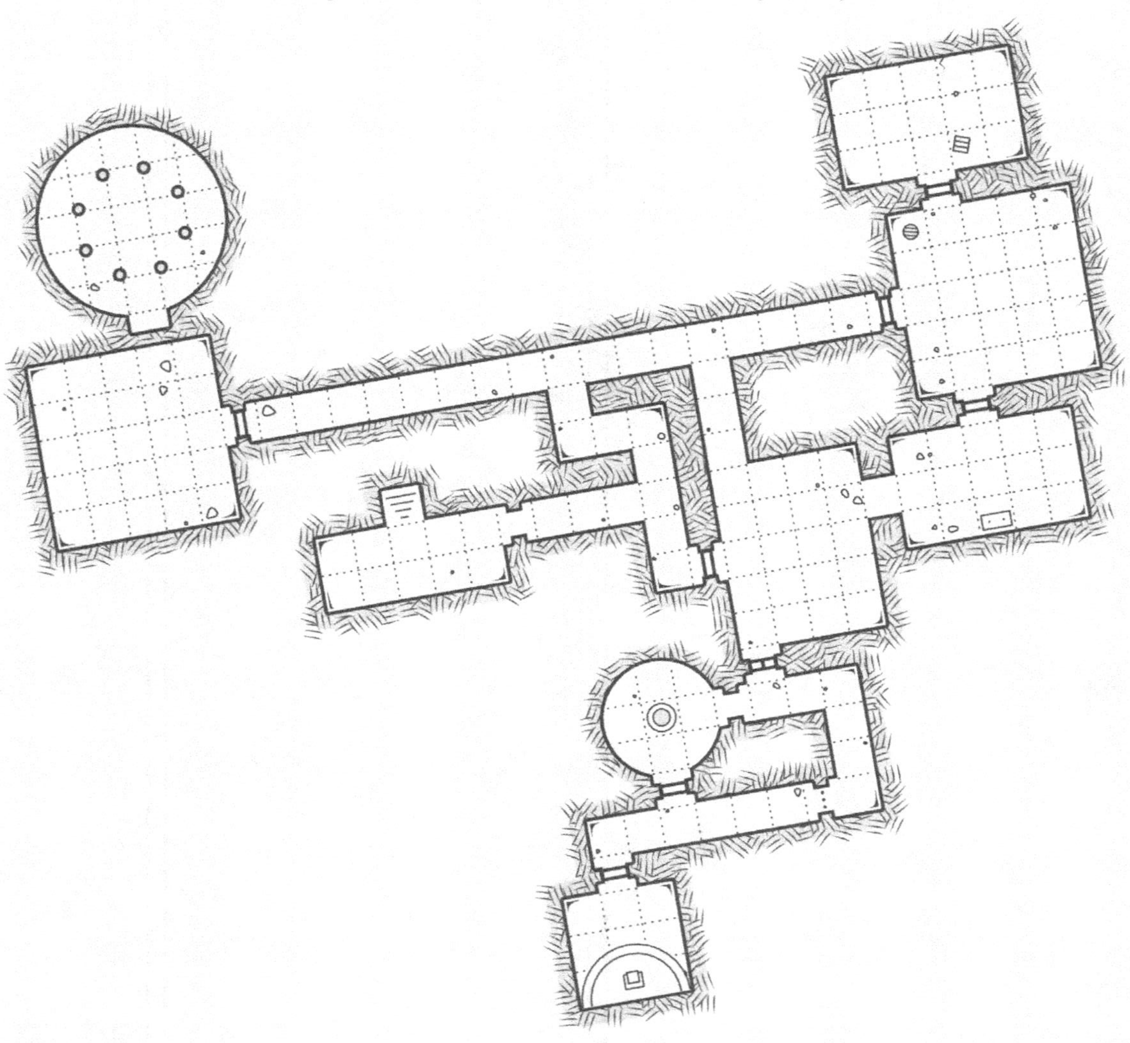

Location: Faction:

Illumination: Temperature:

Architecture:

Plot Hook:

History:

Inhabitants:

Points of Interest:

Abbey of the Golden Titan

After being destroyed by a great flood a long time ago the abbey of the Golden Titan remained abandoned. Recently an undead chimera has made its lair here.

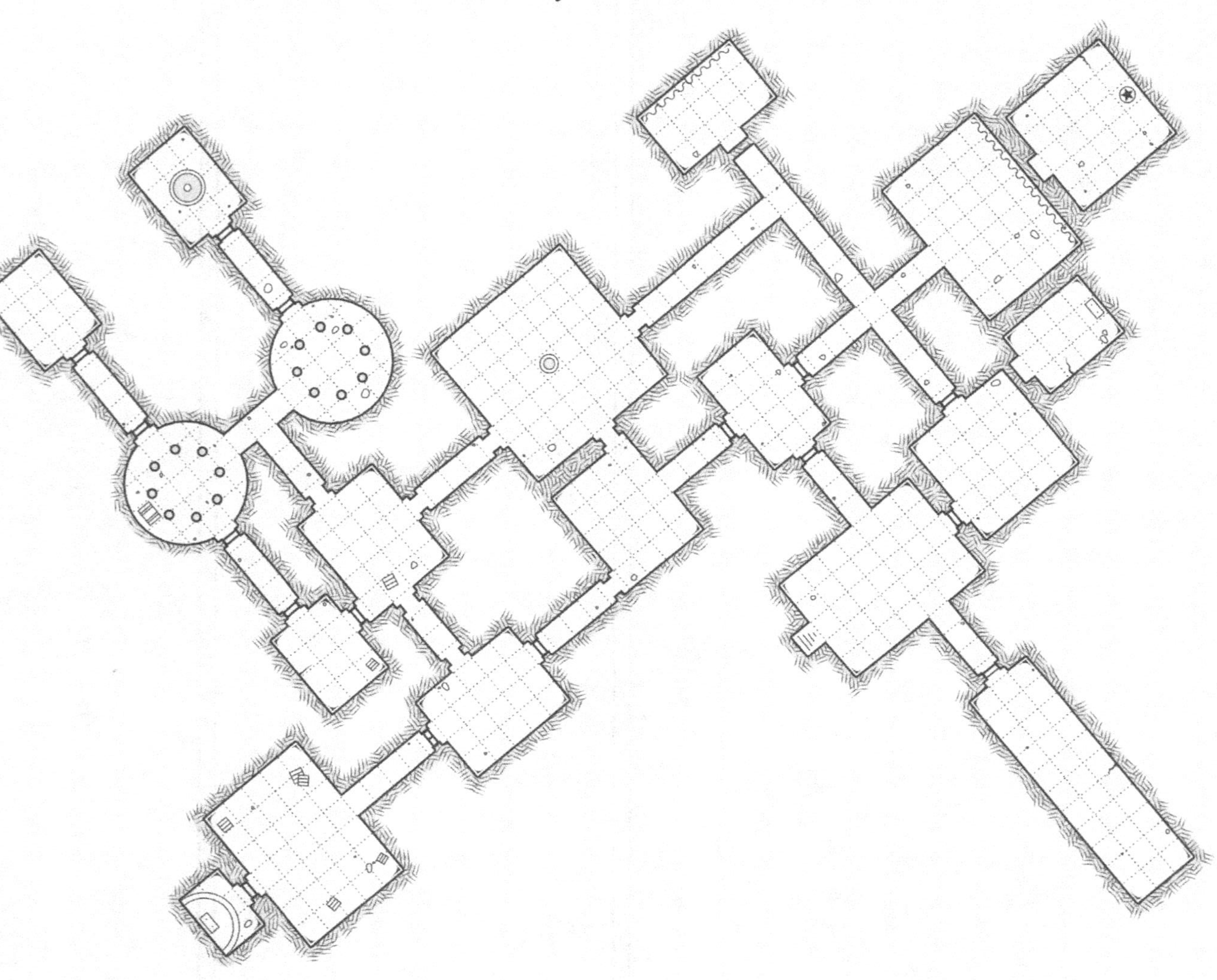

Location:

Faction:

Illumination:

Temperature:

Architecture:

Plot Hook:

History:

Inhabitants:

Points of Interest:

Temple of Damnoryseis

After the fall of Damnoryseis the temple has changed hands many times. These days it is badly infested by pigeons.

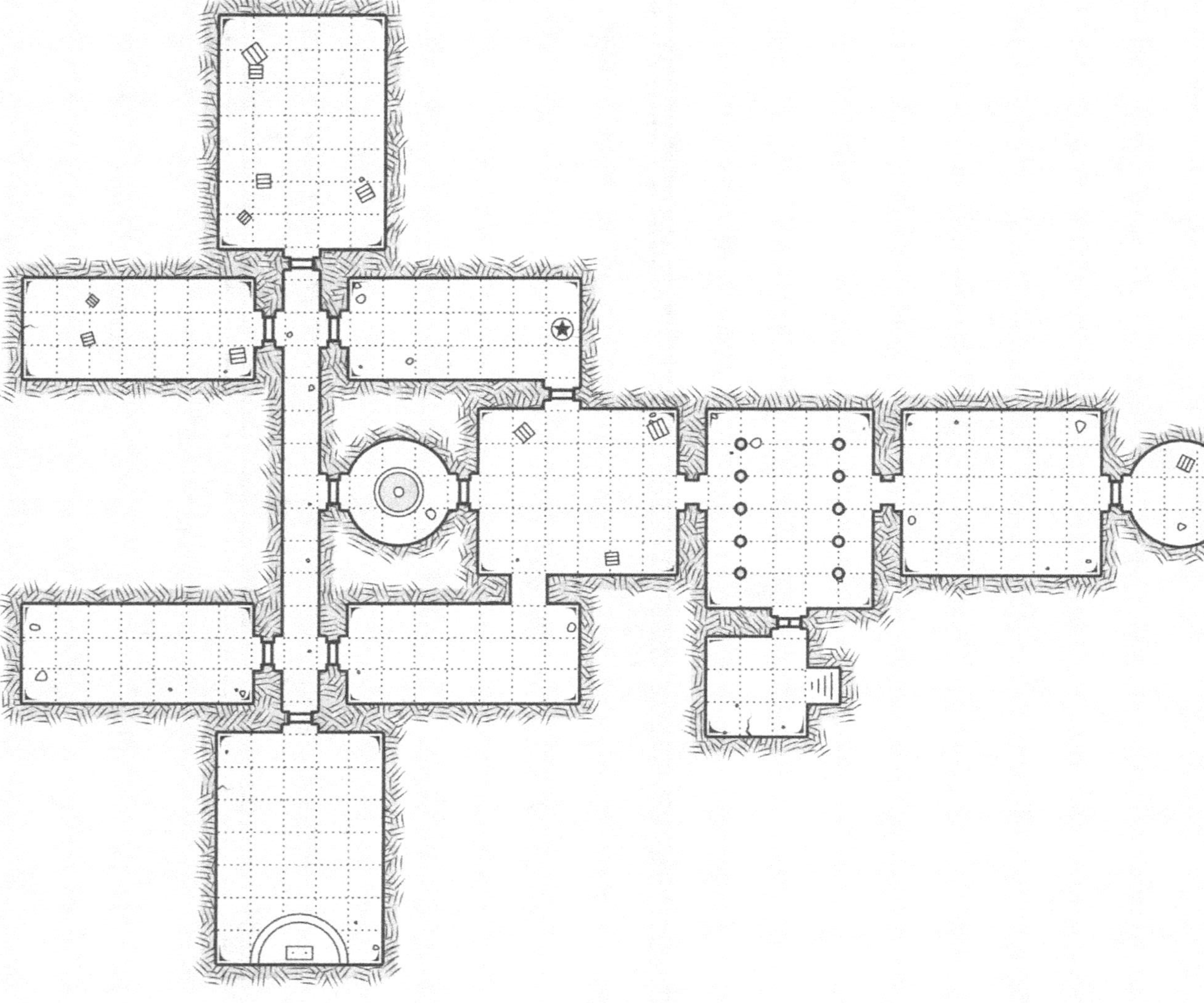

Location:	Faction:
Illumination:	Temperature:

Architecture:

Plot Hook:

History:

Inhabitants:

Points of Interest:

Ruined Palace of the Spider God

After being destroyed by a horrible storm several centuries ago the palace of the Spider God remained abandoned. These days it is badly infested by lions, which don't care about the history of the place.

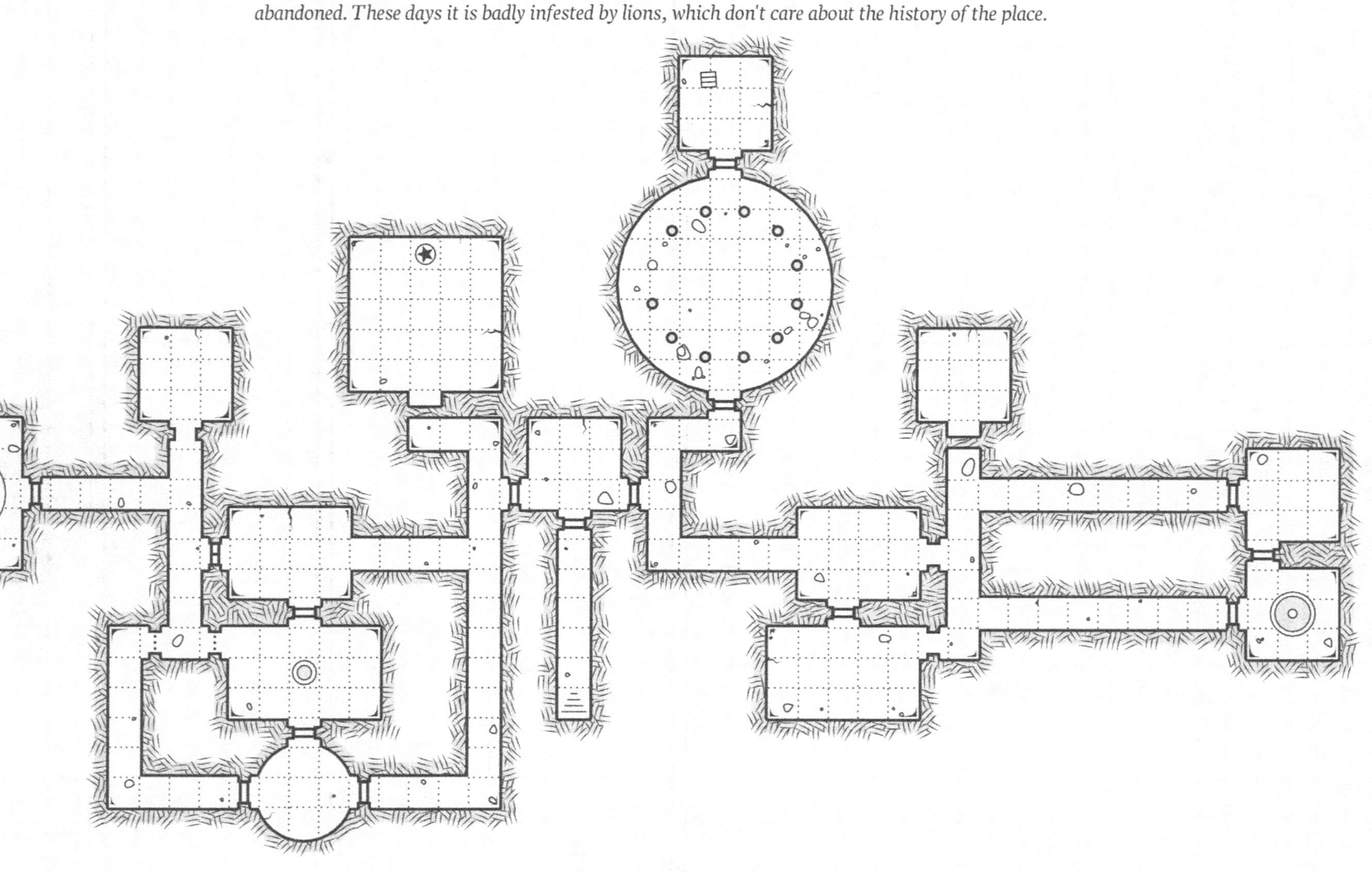

Location:	Faction:
Illumination:	Temperature:
Architecture:	
Plot Hook:	

History:

Inhabitants:

Points of Interest:

Upper Labyrinth of the Blood Lady

The labyrinth of the Blood Lady is situated deep in the frozen lands, protected by the impassable terrain. Currently it is infested by snakes, indifferent to the history of the place. Rumors say that Severi, a legendary niddle, is hidden here.

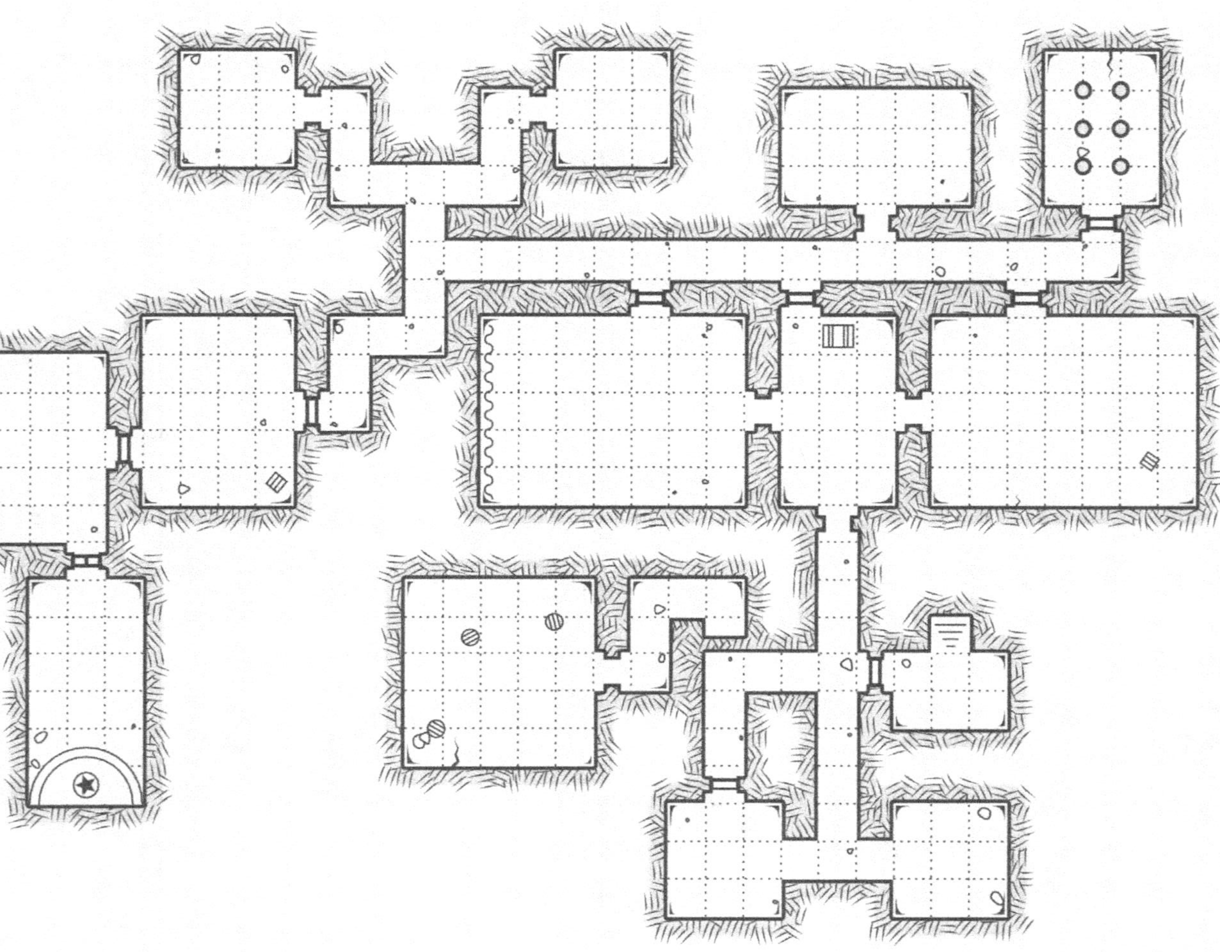

Location:	Faction:
Illumination:	Temperature:
Architecture:	
Plot Hook:	

History:

Inhabitants:

Points of Interest:

Abbey of the Amber King

After being destroyed by a great earthquake several centuries ago the abbey of the Amber King remained abandoned. Lately it was squatted by a gang of goblins. The abbey of the Amber King is a place of growth of a highly valued specie of fungi.

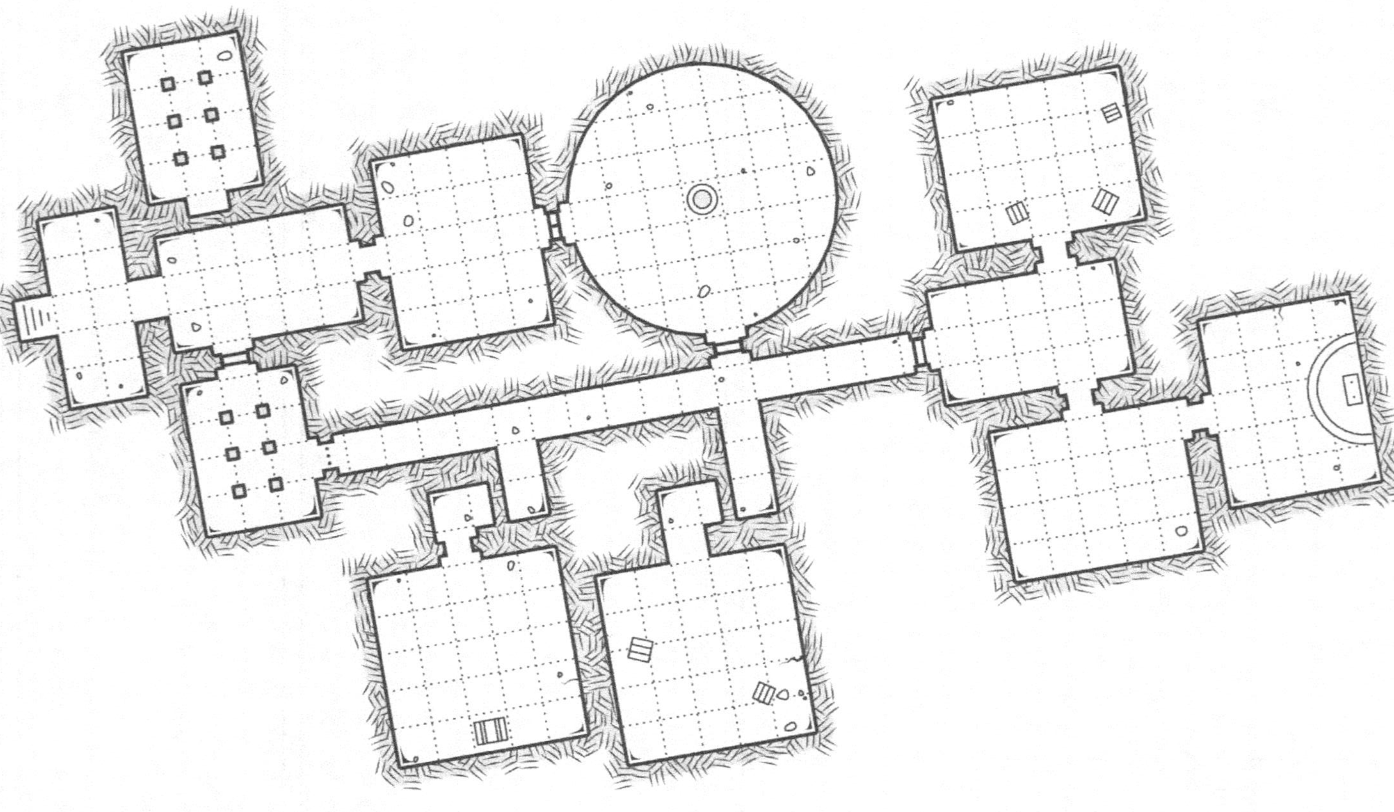

Location:	Faction:
Illumination:	Temperature:

Architecture:

Plot Hook:

History:

Inhabitants:

Points of Interest:

Twilight Maze of Fire

For centuries the maze remained sealed. Recently a huge dragon has made its lair here. The maze is home to a valuable specie of flowers.

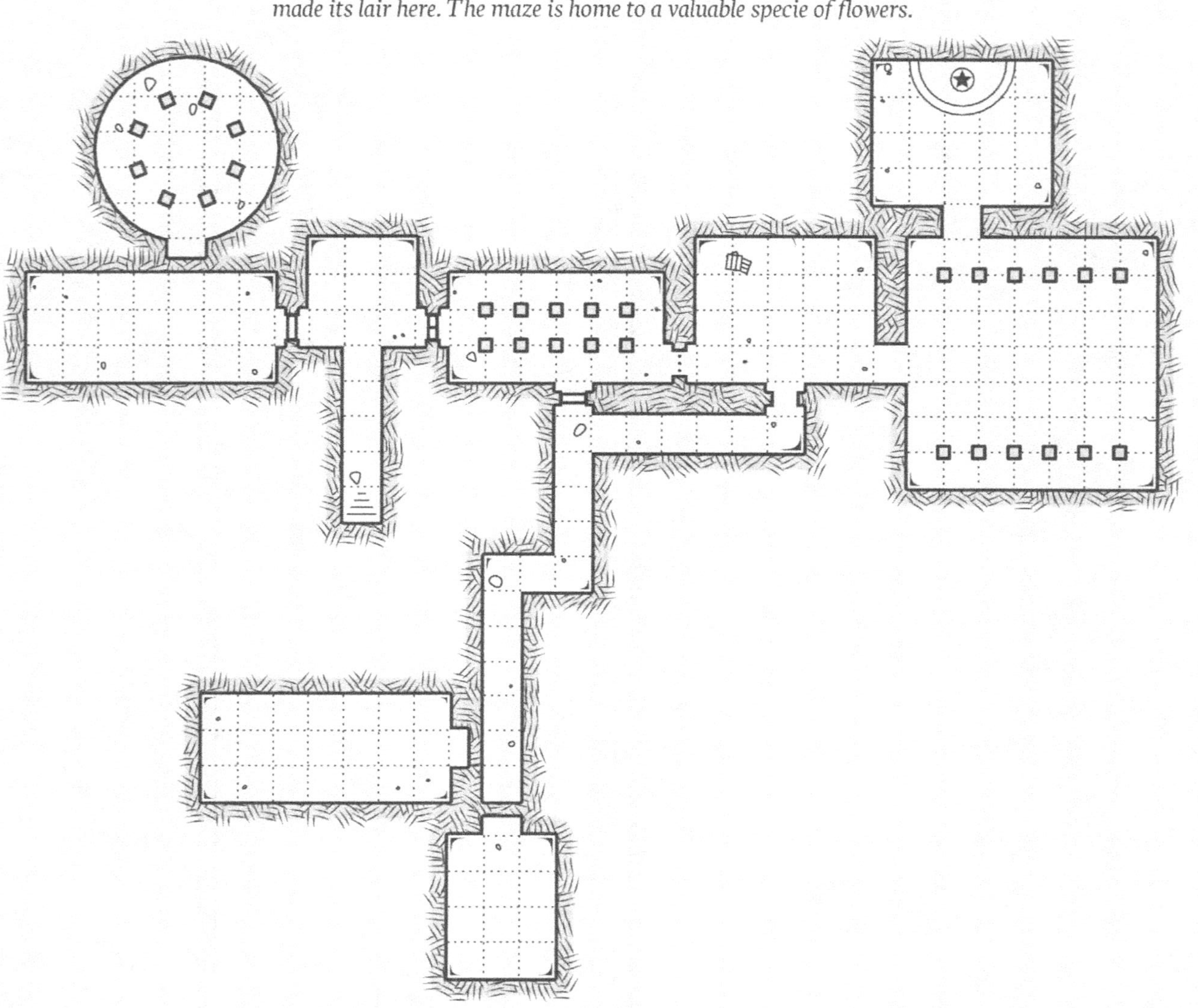

Location:	Faction:
Illumination:	Temperature:
Architecture:	
Plot Hook:	

History:

Inhabitants:

Points of Interest:

Temple of Sevra

After being destroyed by a great arcane disaster a long time ago the temple of Sevra remained abandoned. Recently a gang of orcs rediscovered it, making it their center of operation. The temple of Sevra is home to a highly valued specie of flowers.

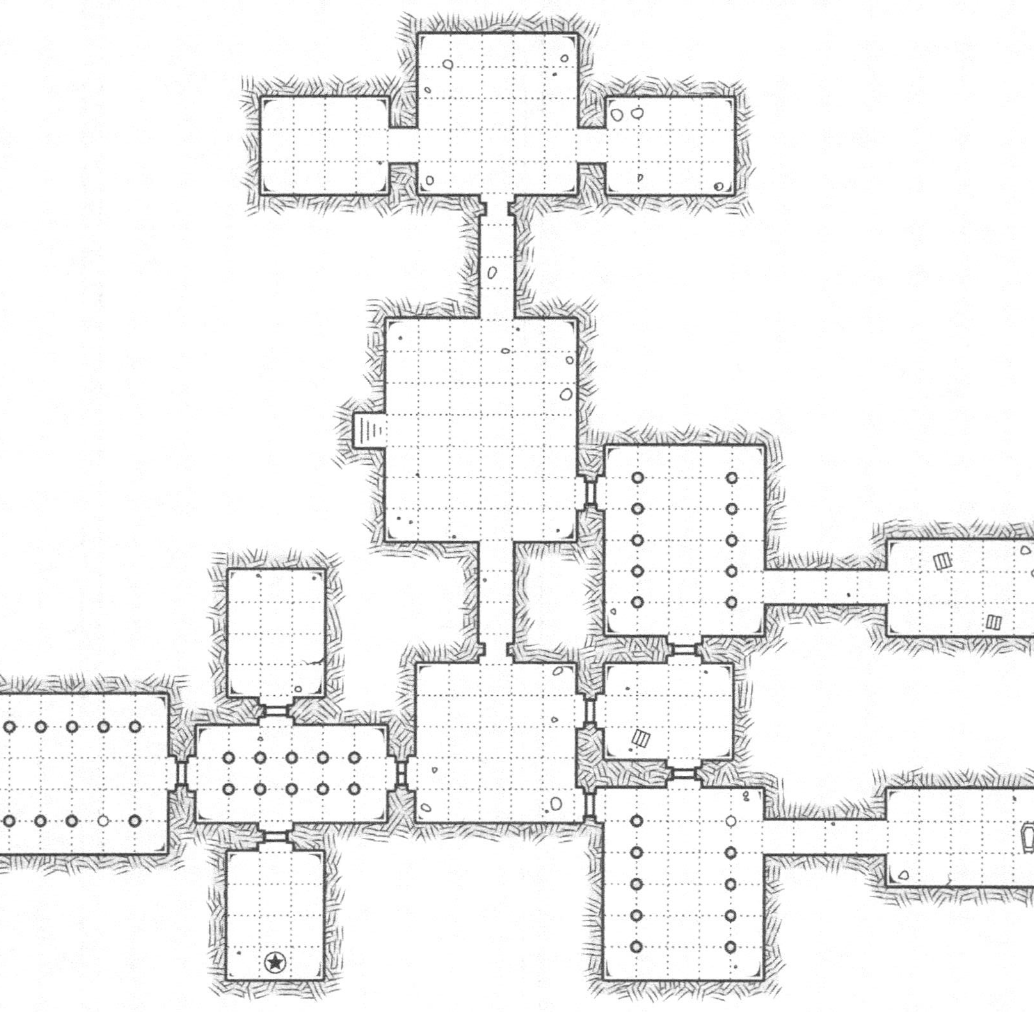

Location: Faction:

Illumination: Temperature:

Architecture:

Plot Hook:

History:

Inhabitants:

Points of Interest:

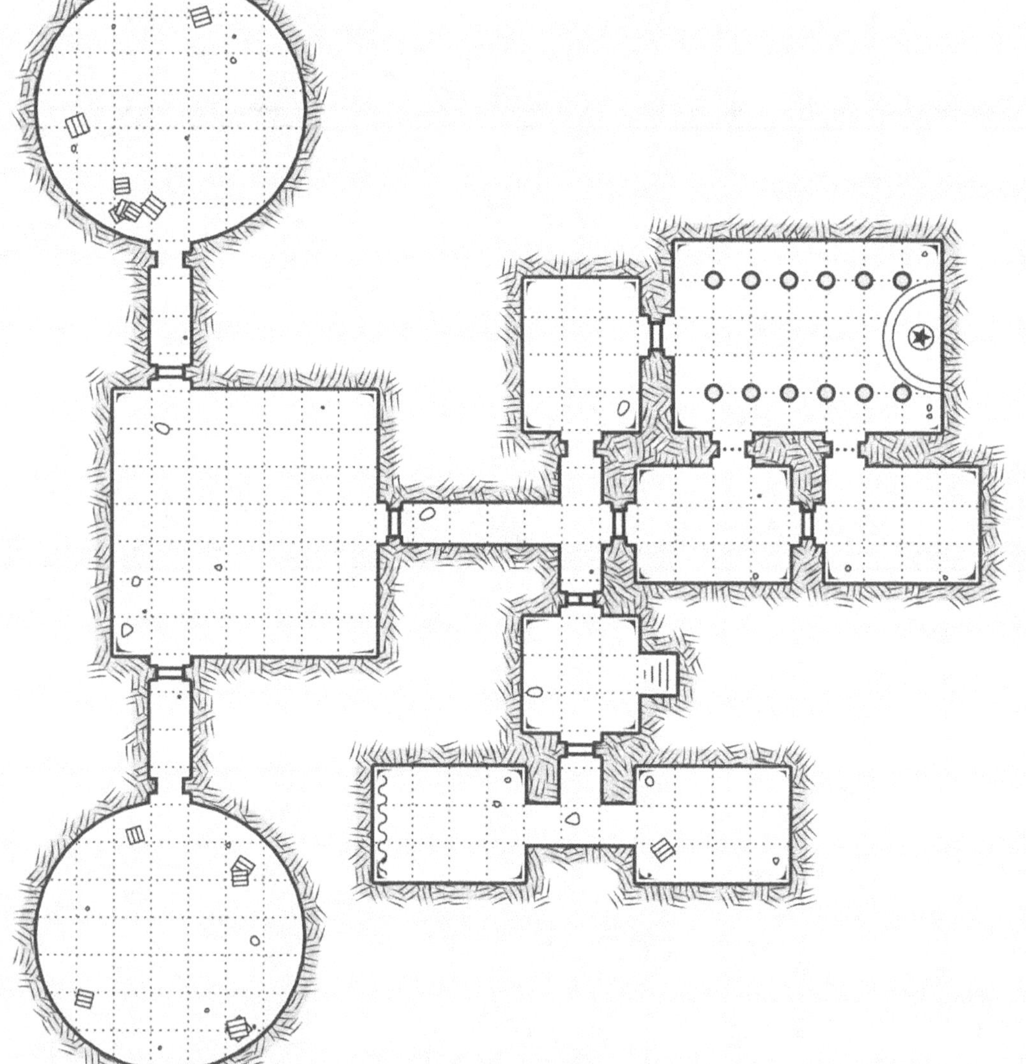

Eternal Den of Hazar

The den of Hazar is situated deep in the dark forest, protected by the harsh weather. Currently it is badly infested by eagles. Word is that the den is rich with gold and magical artifacts.

Location:	Faction:
Illumination:	Temperature:
Architecture:	
Plot Hook:	

History:

Inhabitants:

Points of Interest:

Veiled Monastery of the Red General

After the demise of the Red General the monastery has changed hands many times. Lately it was squatted by a party of orcs. The monastery of the Red General is home to a rare specie of mushrooms.

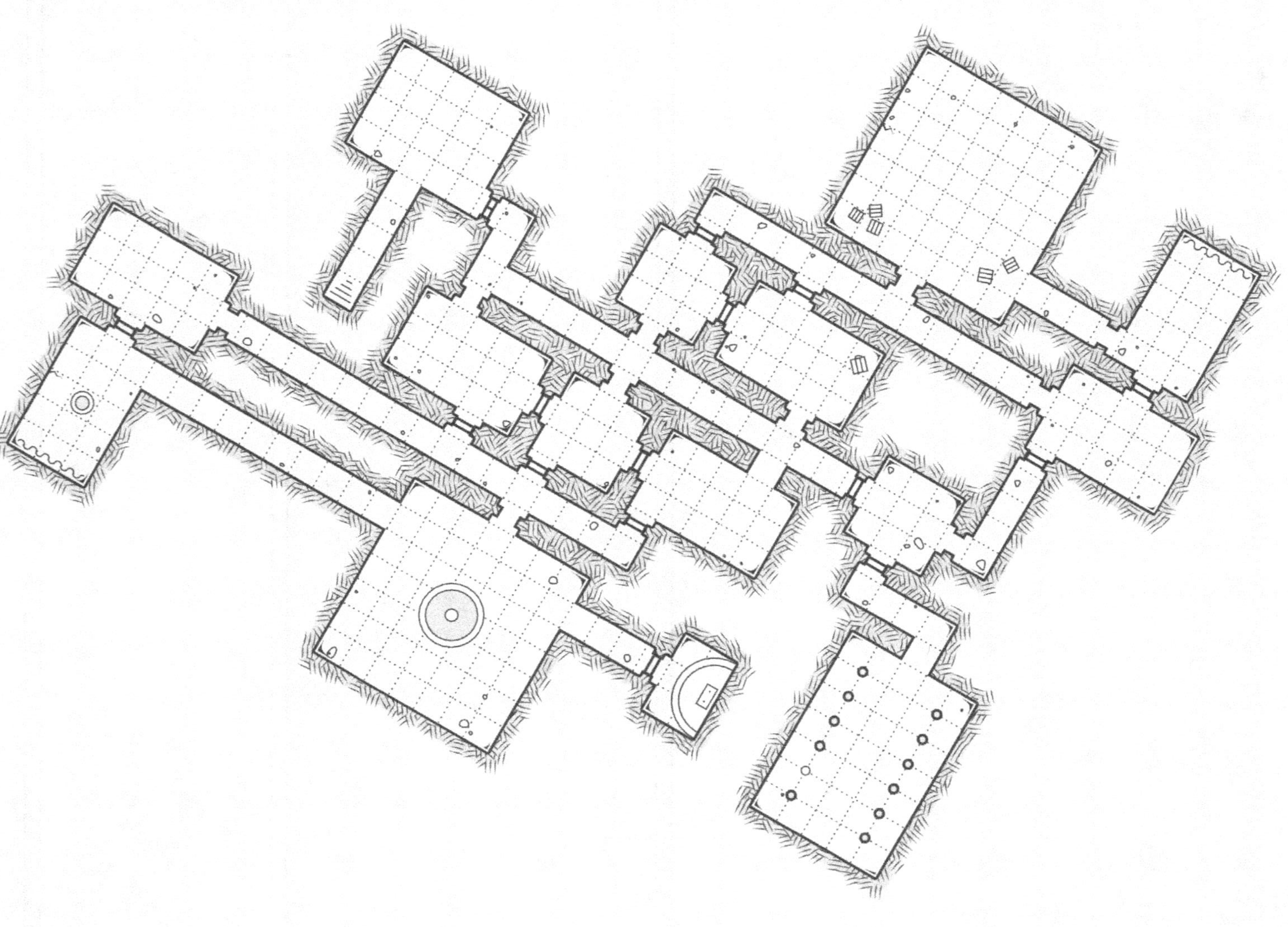

Location: Faction:

Illumination: Temperature:

Architecture:

Plot Hook:

History:

Inhabitants:

Points of Interest:

Catacombs of the Fallen Magus

For a long time the catacombs of the Fallen Magus remained deserted. These days they are infested by rats, which don't care about the history of the place.

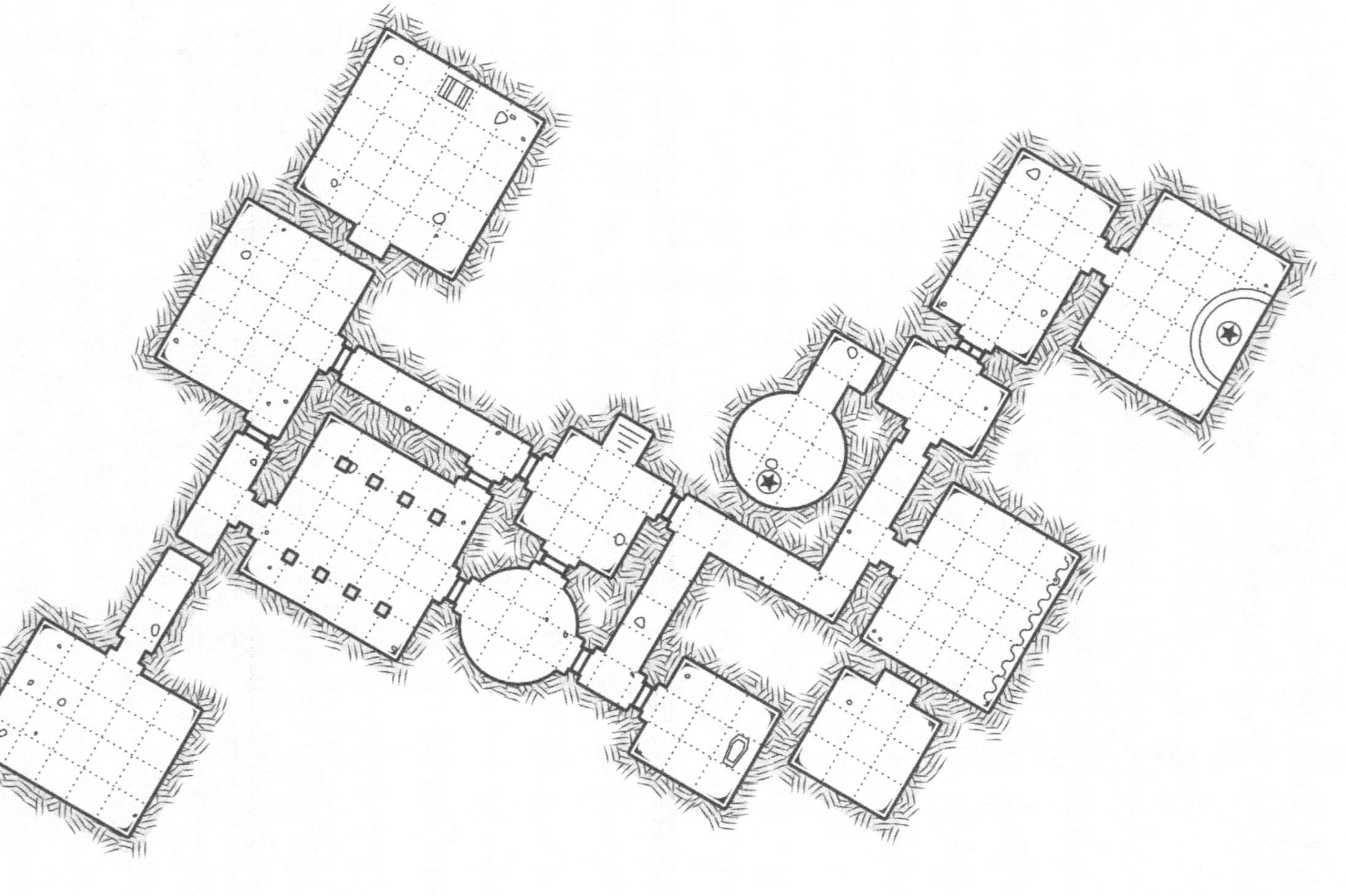

Location:	Faction:
Illumination:	Temperature:
Architecture:	
Plot Hook:	

History:

Inhabitants:

Points of Interest:

Prison of the Golden Baron

After being destroyed by a horrible flood decades ago the prison of the Golden Baron remained uninhabited. These days it is infested by chickens. Rumors say that Mishannos, a legendary lantern, is still hidden here.

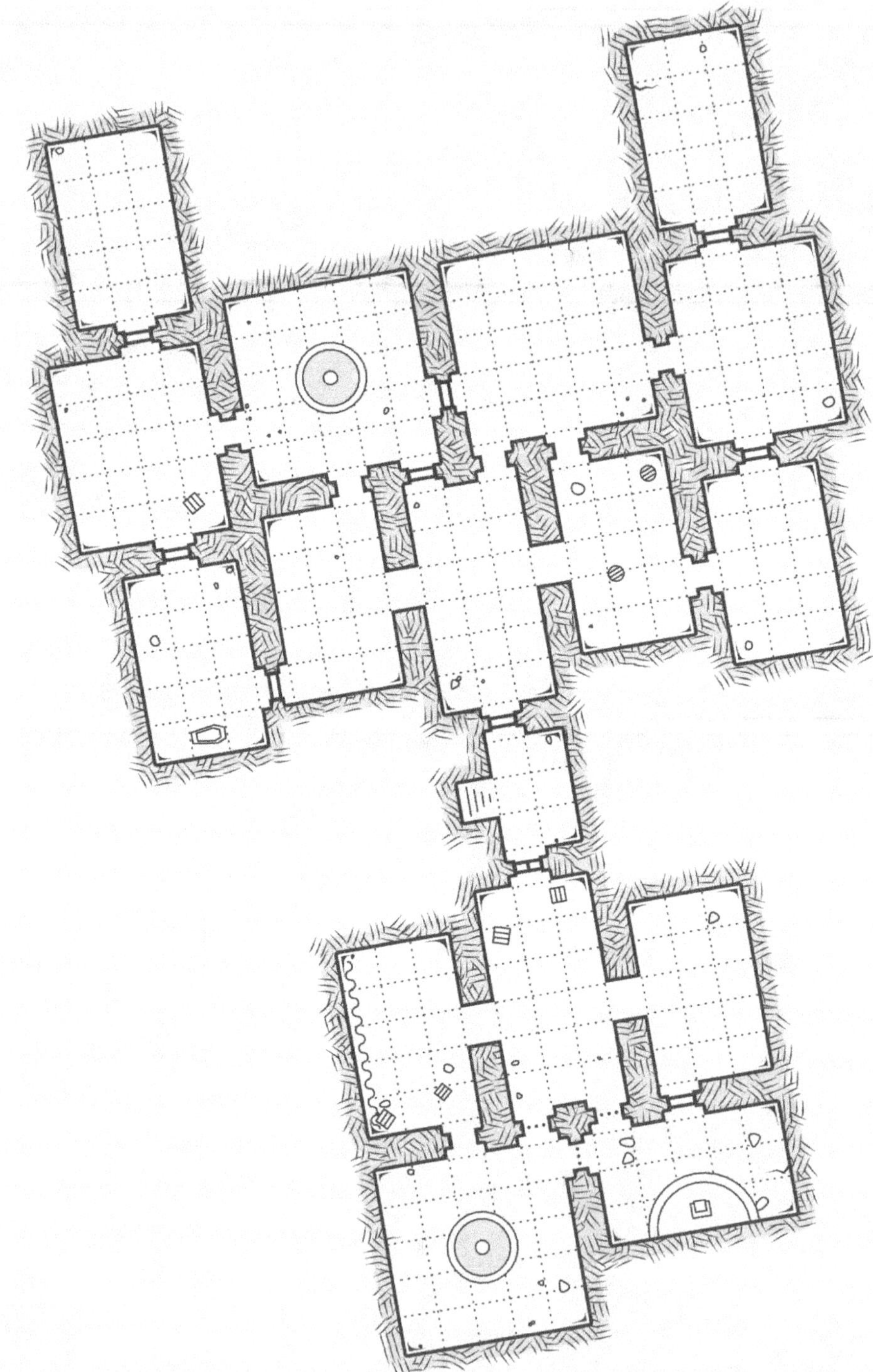

Location:	Faction:
Illumination:	Temperature:
Architecture:	
Plot Hook:	

History:

Inhabitants:

Points of Interest:

Eternal Mansion of the One-eyed Messiah

Long after the One-eyed Messiah's fall the mansion remained deserted. Currently it is infested by crows, indifferent to the history of the place.

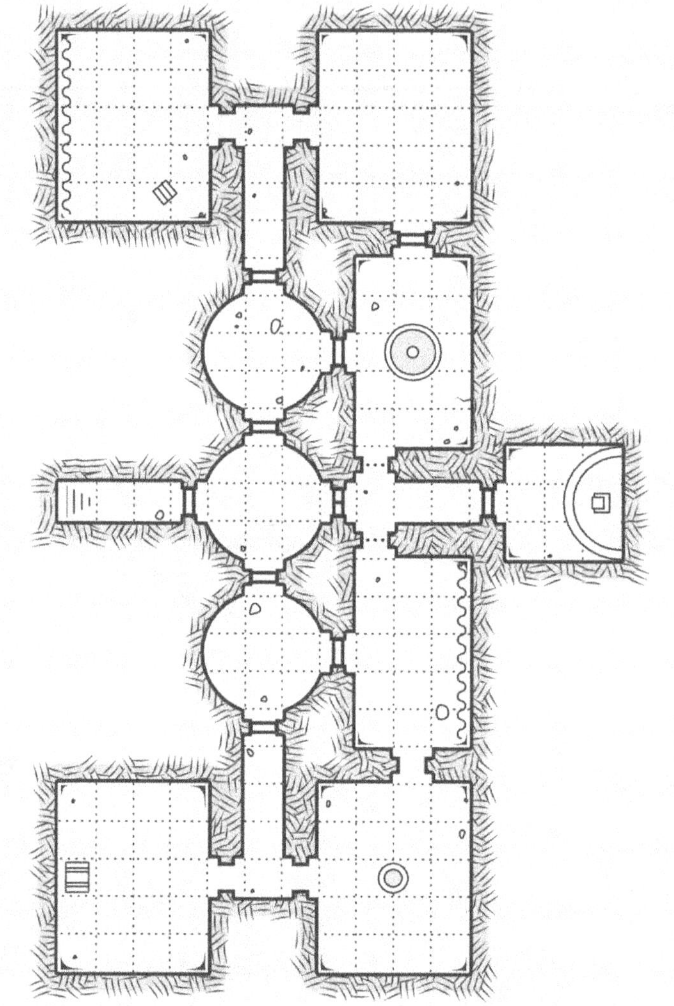

Location: Faction:

Illumination: Temperature:

Architecture:

Plot Hook:

History:

Inhabitants:

Points of Interest:

Catacombs of Haz-Perai

The catacombs of Haz-Perai are situated deep in the swamps, protected by the harsh weather. These days they are infested by wolfs, which don't care about the history of the place. Word is that countless treasures of ancient books and magical artifacts are stored here.

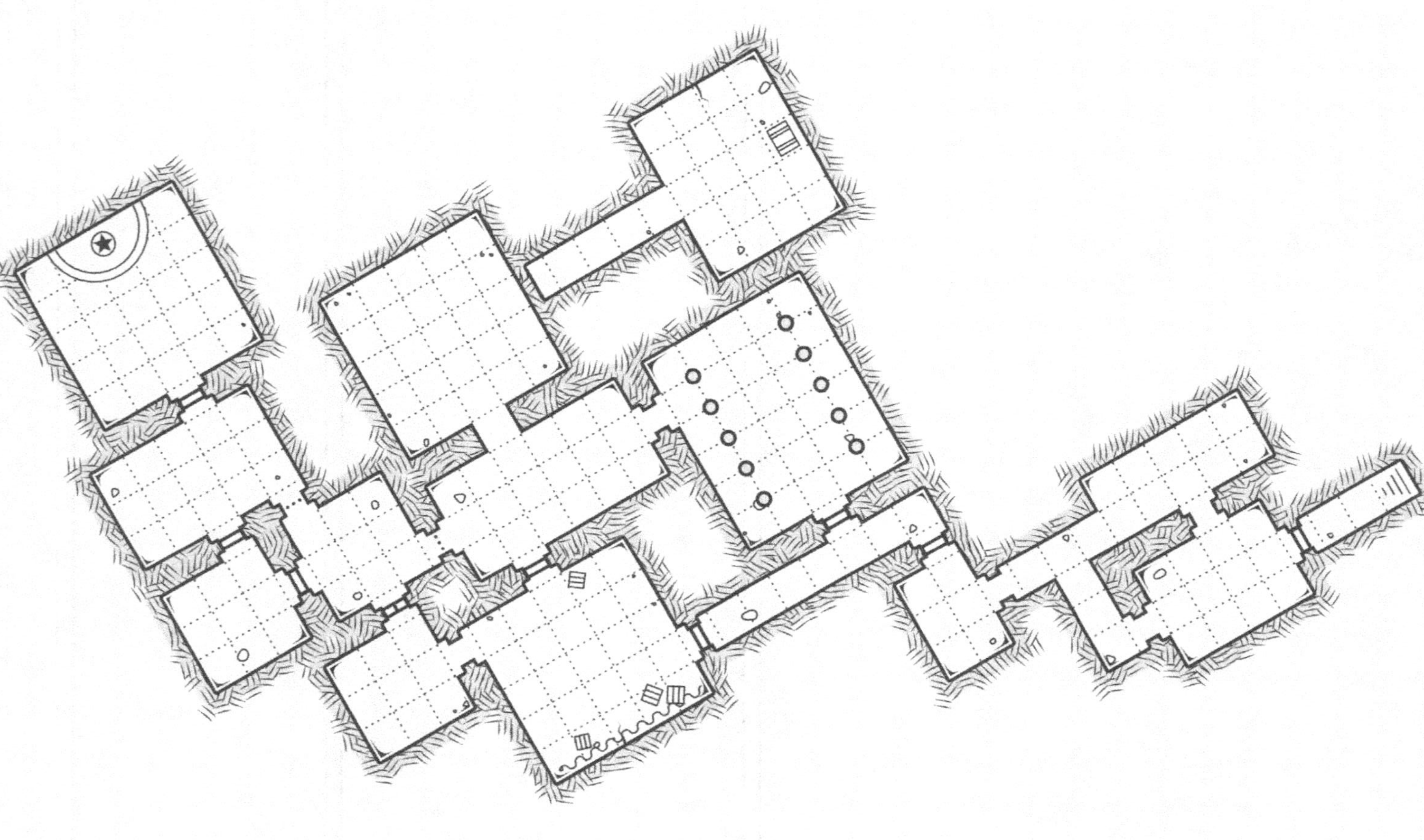

Location:	Faction:
Illumination:	Temperature:
Architecture:	
Plot Hook:	

History:

Inhabitants:

Points of Interest:

Mountain Palace of the Dark God

The palace of the Dark God is situated deep in the forest, far from the nearest town. Lately a band of cultists rediscovered it. It is said that Riellis-Karkemus, a legendary compass, is hidden here.

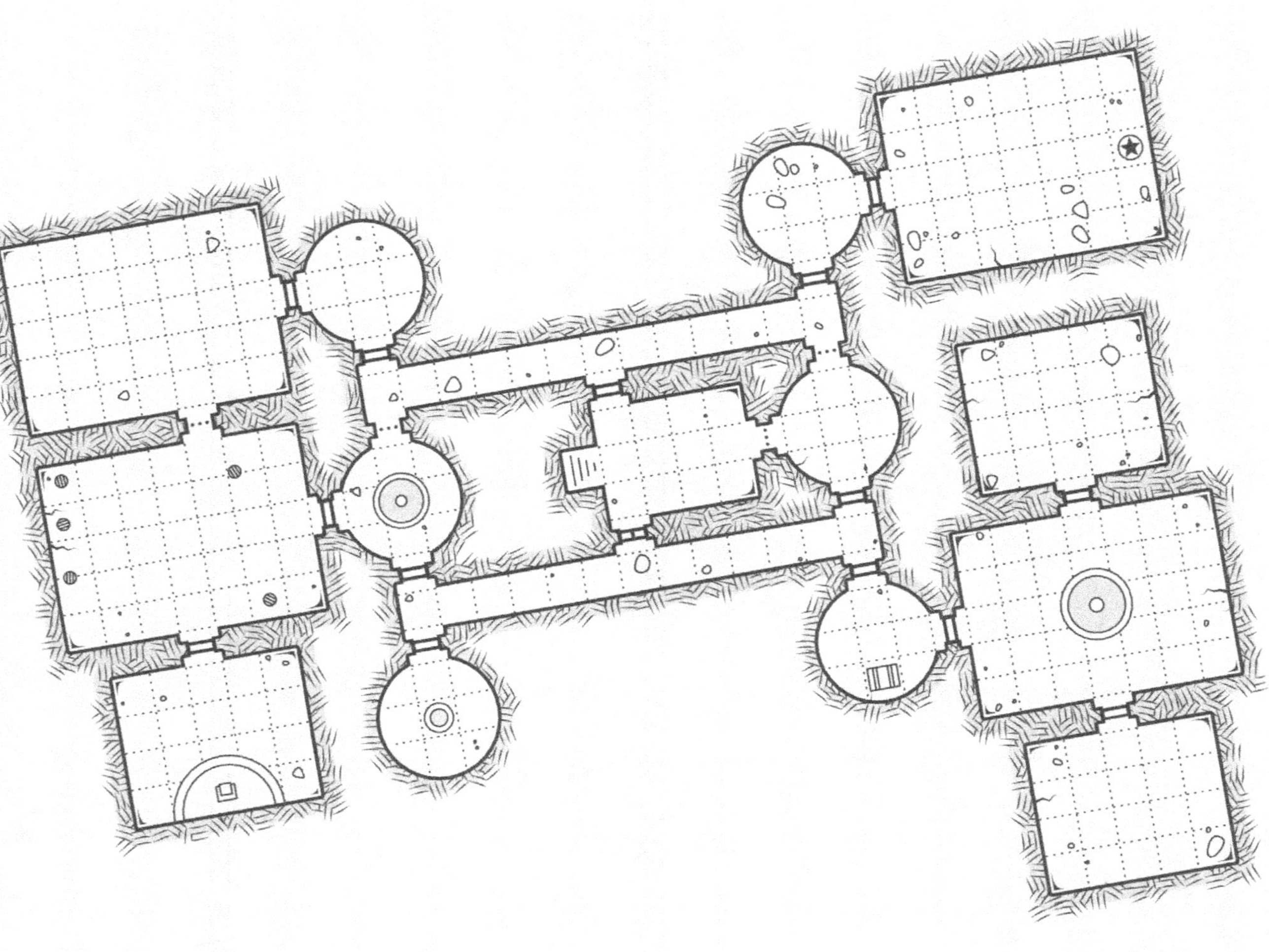

Location:	Faction:
Illumination:	Temperature:
Architecture:	
Plot Hook:	

History:

Inhabitants:

Points of Interest:

Palace of Phelmos

For a long time the palace of Phelmos remained deserted. Lately it was squatted by a party of goblins. The palace of Phelmos is home to a rare specie of herbs.

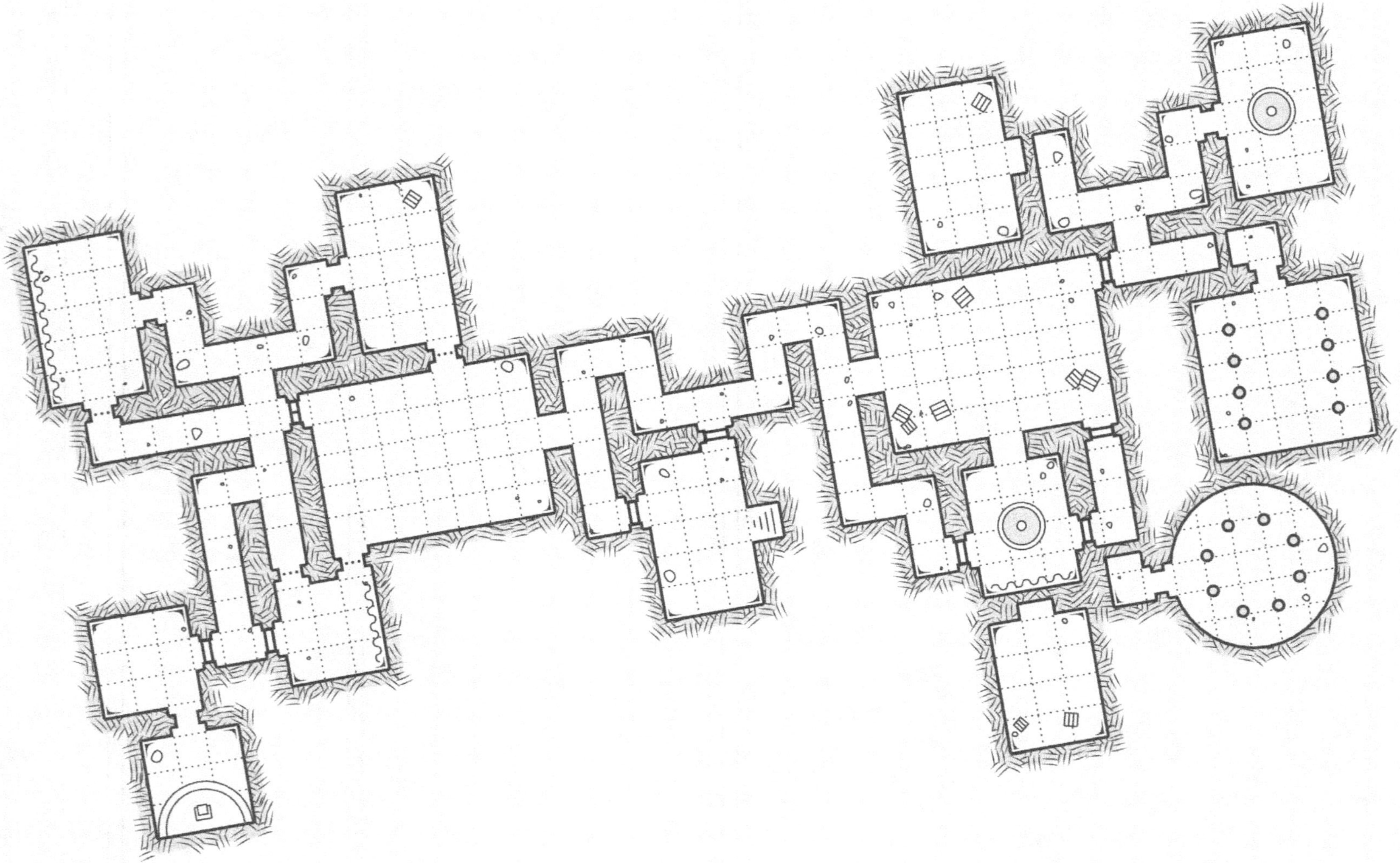

Location:	Faction:
Illumination:	Temperature:
Architecture:	
Plot Hook:	

History:

Inhabitants:

Points of Interest:

Swamp Prison of Dawn Heart

The prison is situated deep in the forest, far from civilization. Lately a terryfying mutant wolf has made its lair here. Word is that Amnos, a legendary blade, is hidden here.

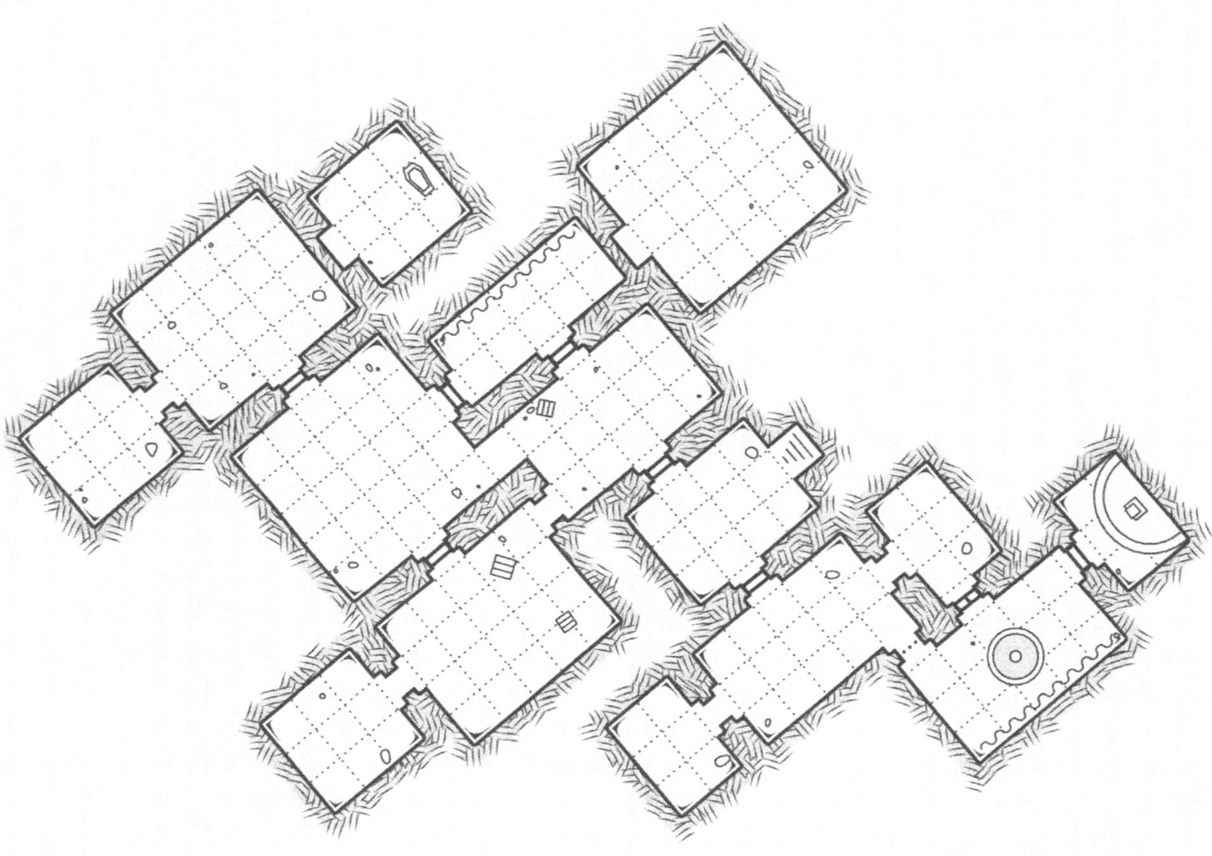

<table>
<tr><td>Location:</td><td>Faction:</td></tr>
<tr><td>Illumination:</td><td>Temperature:</td></tr>
<tr><td colspan="2">Architecture:</td></tr>
<tr><td colspan="2">Plot Hook:</td></tr>
</table>

History:

Inhabitants:

Points of Interest:

Eternal Monastery of the Vampire Master

*The monastery of the Vampire Master is situated deep in the marshes,
protected by the dangerous local fauna. These days it is infested by ants.*

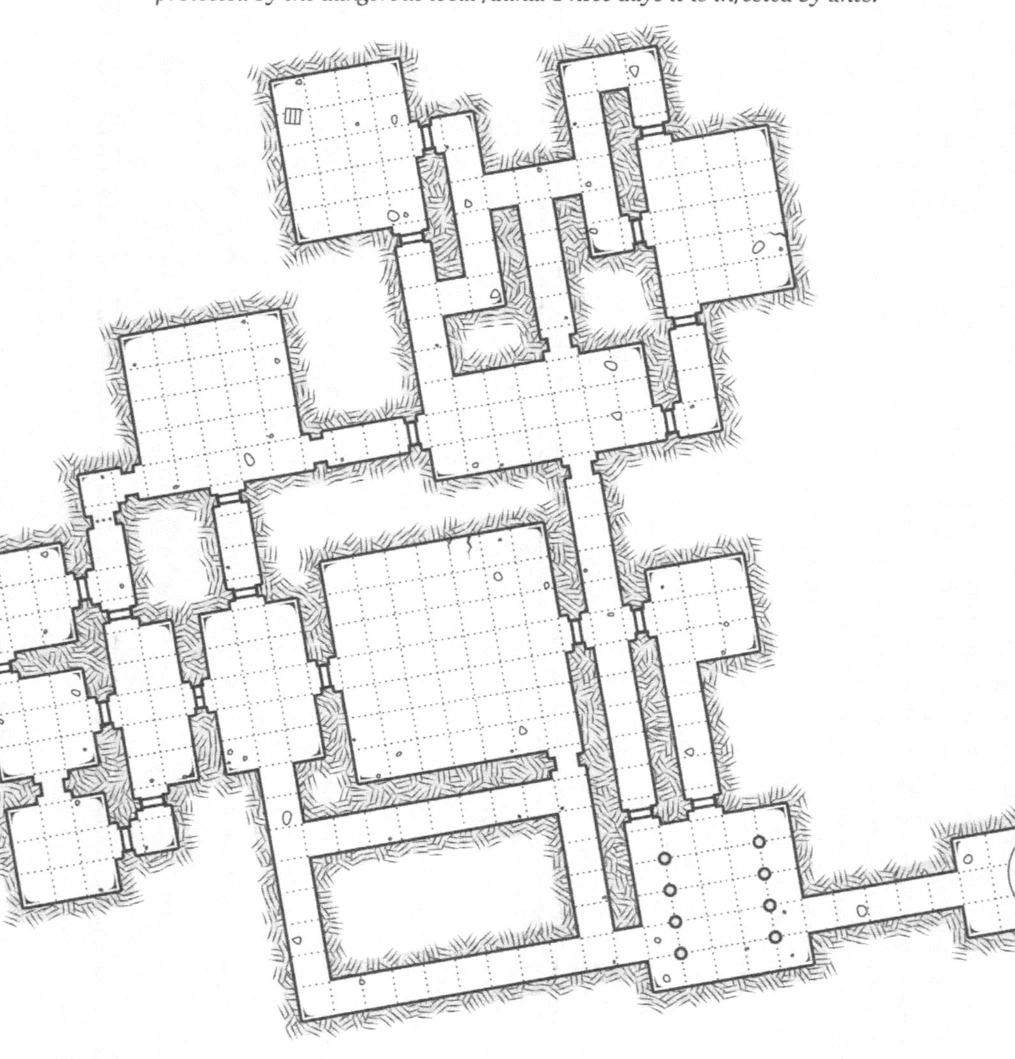

Location:	Faction:
Illumination:	Temperature:
Architecture:	
Plot Hook:	

History:

Inhabitants:

Points of Interest:

Nightring Monastery

The monastery is situated deep in the forest, far from civilization. Lately it was squatted by a band of kobolds. It is said that the monastery is rich with treasures of ancient books and magical artifacts.

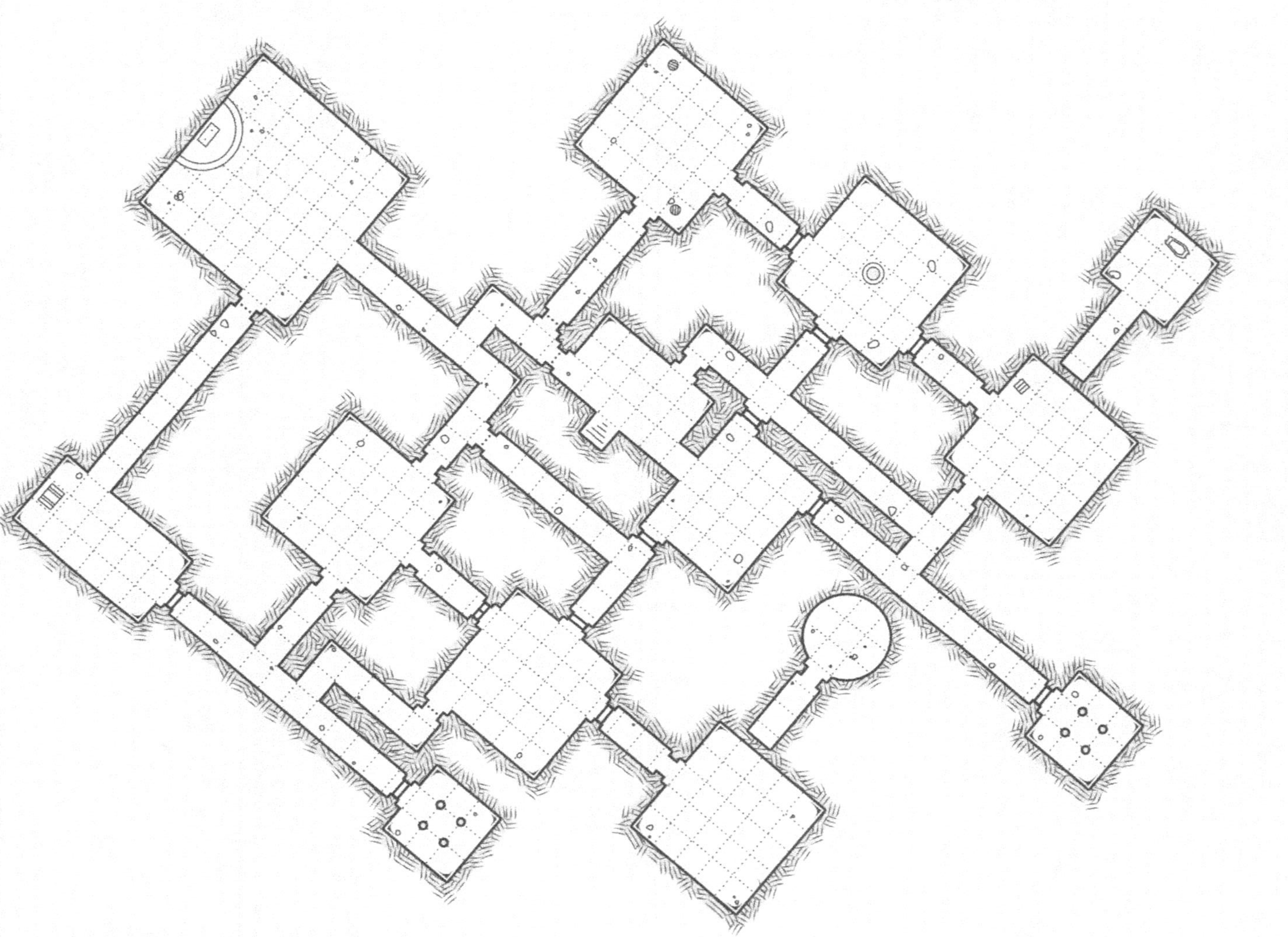

Location: Faction:

Illumination: Temperature:

Architecture:

Plot Hook:

History:

Inhabitants:

Points of Interest:

Hidden Labyrinth of the Void Prince

After being destroyed by a horrible storm several centuries ago the labyrinth of the Void Prince remained abandoned. Currently it is badly infested by eagles. It is rumored that the labyrinth is rich with gold and magical artifacts.

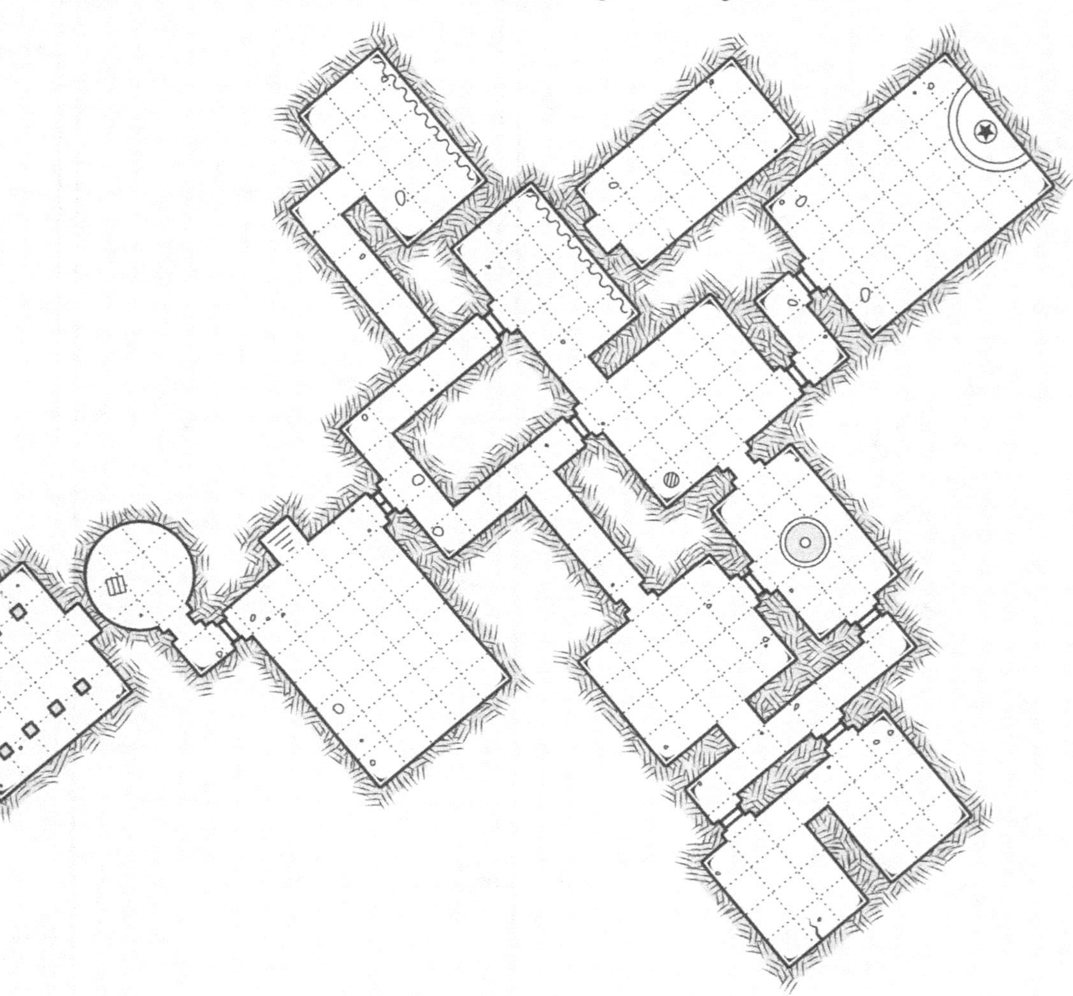

Location:	Faction:
Illumination:	Temperature:
Architecture:	
Plot Hook:	

History:

Inhabitants:

Points of Interest: